MIND YOUR THOUGHTS

Words Of Wisdom

HIS HOLINESS SHRI AASAANJI

INDIA • SINGAPORE • MALAYSIA

ISBN 979-8-89066-915-5

His Holiness
Shri Aasaanji

World Renowned, Non-Religious, Contemporary Spiritual
Leader, Global Humanitarian, a Great Visionary and Living
Enlightened Master of Inner-Science & Ancient wisdom.

Founder of the Atmayoga Foundation - One Human Family
(An Institute for Inner-Science and Self-Transformation),
Guruji is globally known as a practical spiritualist
spreading Global Peace through Inner-Peace.

www.atmayoga.in

CONTENTS

Contents

PREFACE

It is customary part of primary schooling to study the human body, all its components, and their respective functions. Irrespective of the curriculum or the language used for the study, anyone who has ever been to school, at least primary school, would not escape these topics. And, just as the geographical and / or political maps of the world, and the respective countries adorn the walls, no classroom is complete without a similar map of the human body, displaying the organs that are a part of it. An average student is capable of pointing out most of the major organs that enable us to live and function in this world.

However, is there a map or a chart of the human body that points out to us a very critical component that impact our daily lives – "The Human Mind" - the non-physical power within the physical body? And yet, it is such an inherent part of what and who we are, is it not ? Hardly a day may pass in the life of any individual where there is no mention of this wonderful thing called "Mind"!

"Make up your mind"; "Change your mind"; "Give the mind a break"; "Be in the right frame of mind"; "Don't let the mind wander"; "Out of your mind"; "Take the weight of the mind"; "There's a picture in the mind"; "A mind of his / it's own"......!!

The mind seems to be such a critical driver of the human existence, but yet such an amorphous, intangible thing! There is so much that is known about the mind, and yet the more that is known, the more the intrigue and questions! We don't, however, shy away from classifying it, giving it many different definitions and ascribing to it major functions that define our existence. We liberally use terms like 'conscious mind', 'sub-conscious mind', and 'un-conscious mind', without really knowing where they exist and in what form.

Though not a clearly defined organ in our body, we believe that the mind is something that has an amorphous existence within us, possibly shifting shapes often; redefining and recasting itself into different moulds and manifesting itself through the various actions that we indulge in. We also use the term "Mental", in association with the mind, which the dictionary describes as "relating to the mind, or involving the process of thinking".

We can extrapolate the term "thinking" to mean several related or sub-processes such as observing, knowing, thinking, reasoning, feeling, wishing, imagining, remembering, judging, thereby expanding the gamut of processes that are related to the mind. Or, alternatively we could surmise that the "Mind" is, in fact, a sum total of all these processes that we perform with the brain, which results in the creation / production of information that the brain uses to further indulge in these processes. The complexities underpinning these led to the emergence of a field of study, Psychology, which was defined in the late 19th century as «the science of mental life, both of its phenomena and their conditions".

The definition seeks to cover a wide range of issues regarding the very intangible, and amorphous thing called the mind, indicating that the "mind" is something that can be perceived, observed, studied, and worked upon, through the processes that it consists and the impact that it brings about on the human existence.

Right from the ancient civilizations of Egypt, India, China, Greece, and Persia, and right through the middle ages, and renaissance, and to the neuroscience theories and experiments of this day, the "mind" has always been on the top of everyone's mind!! From philosophy to religion to the modern medical sciences, it has been an object of immense interest, in a drive to uncover its mechanisms, map its functioning, and control the manner in which it influences human behaviour and its consequences.

There is no major work on philosophy or spirituality that does not delve into the depths of how the mind works, and how thoughts are the fundamental basis of existence and manifestation. From The Holy Bible, and The Qur'an and the teachings of Confucius, to the vast expanse of philosophy propounded via the Bhagavad Gita, the Upanishads, Shiva Sutras and Thirumandiram, to Buddha's teachings propounded by the Dhammapada, and more ancient yet contemporary philosophical treatises like the Thirukkural, there is no major civilizational view that does not speak on the nature of thoughts, and how they are susceptible to the universe's influence, as well as how we can control these influences and their manifestations.

So, therefore, it turns out that there are many ways we can adopt to adapt the mind in such a way that it is one with the universe and in perfect resonance with it, which is critical to the attainment of peace, that brings in its wake, happiness, success and achievements. *Mind Your Thoughts,* takes you through a journey on what is the nature of thoughts that inhabit the mind, how they manifest us in this universe, and how to get a handle on these thoughts and convert them into tools that can shape our destinies. The book provides a simple pathway to appreciate the power of the mind, use it to shape our existence in the way that we want, and progress towards our chosen goals and objectives.

The intent of the book is to convey in the simplest terms that we are the masters of our destinies and not any external or unknown forces, and how it is well within our control to take charge of our peace, happiness and success. By breaking the shackles of our innate self-doubts we can always achieve what we wanted to. When we understand how our thoughts are shaping our actions, and appreciate the power that we possess to control and manage the thoughts, our dreams are well within our reach.

Mind Your Thoughts will demystify the workings of the mind and help people to find the right path that is unique to each self, driven by the understanding that each person is unique in the eyes of the supreme, and illustrates that it is in the hands of every individual to commune with the supreme. Such commune will lead the way to a more peaceful existence, not only for the individual, but also contributes to a peaceful world inhabited by a happy humanity.

It is with immense pleasure that I present this book to the world, as an offering that will serve to enhance the power of humanity, and as a humble contribution to a peaceful world.

Aham Brahmasmi!

– Atmayogi Shri Aasaanji

IT'S ALL IN THE MIND!

Believe in yourself!

You can achieve only what your mind can conceive
And You can only conceive what you believe!

It is divine nature that your end results can
never exceed your self-story,

Because the universe favours only those who
believe in themselves!

No matter how much you believe in others,
or how much ever others believe in you,
You can never achieve anything unless
you believe in yourself!

– His Holiness Shri Aasaanji

Nothing sums up the truth of existence than this statement from the great French mathematician-philosopher Rene Descartes – "Ï think, therefore, I am". Our thoughts are proof of our existence, the clear indicator that we are alive and thriving, and they're the fount of the life energy that courses through us at any point. It is hard to separate out a moment in our existence when we were not thinking. Thoughts occur or manifest in several ways - Belief, attitudes, perceptions, worries, goals, the will, satisfaction, faith & prayers, and even the dreams, when we're relinquishing consciousness wilfully.

If it is the existence of thoughts that confirm our existence in this universe, it is the very same thoughts that also define the nature of our existence. They are what makes us who we are, and provide the framework for how we relate to others and to the universe. They are not just a mere proof of existence, not just a reminder of why we are humans, and not just an indicator of why we are different from the other beings in this universe. Our thoughts form the fundamental framework that drives our actions on a day-to-day basis.

> ***"All that we are is a result of what we have thought. It is founded on our thoughts. It is made up of our thoughts"***
>
> ***– Dhammapada***

Our thoughts are indications of how our inner being receives, interprets and processes the sensations that we receive from the universe around us. For example, while walking through a busy road, a child would find herself drawn towards a pushcart selling ice-cream & candies, while her mother might see that as an unnecessary distraction on the way, and a passerby in a car might consider the cart a needless obstruction blocking flow of traffic. Every moment of our existence is filled with several such stimuli, which make us react consciously or unconsciously, driving other related thoughts and actions, creating newer thoughts, moulding existing ones, pushing or pulling us in different directions, moving us closer to or farther away from our chosen goals and destinations.

This is an unmistakable fact of each of our inherent natures, intimately connected to our existence in this universe. Every day, during the course of existence, we are exposed to these stimuli unconsciously, in the thousands, from the moment we awaken to the moment we lose consciousness in our sleep, and even beyond that. The hurried glance at the morning's headlines in the day's newspaper or the soothing or jarring music that probably wafts in from the neighbourhood, the chatter from the television early in the morning, or the innumerable messages that are jumping out at us from the multitude of social media applications, each of these daring us to look away but subtly and benignly enticing us into their realm of influence, spinning off thoughts and more thoughts inside our heads, setting off trains that are headed in several directions, overwhelming our attention, and most of the time succeeding in enslaving it, at the cost of other inputs or notes or notices that we may have lined up for action. And each of these trains start taking a life of their own, when we start piloting them in consonance with the thoughts of other people who we come in contact with, hurtling at high speed, demanding more involvement to ensure that they do not run into accidents that could find a path back to us and cause harm or disruption.

If we pause for a moment, it will become immensely clear to us as to how this storm of stimuli really overwhelms existing thought processes, stacking up a lot of **unsolicited thoughts** inside us, at times driving unplanned actions which also end up not only disrupting well laid out plans and actions, but also impacting beliefs and notions - thoughts that we hold at the core of our existence.

The sensations that our being receives from the moment of our birth, start shaping our innate beliefs about ourselves, the people around us, and the big wide and ever-changing universe. The beliefs drive our attitudes including who we are and how we relate to other people and their universes. The attitudes in-turn give shape to how we perceive the other objects of creation – people, the beautiful flora & fauna around us, the forces of nature - and above all the actions and events that arise from the existence of all these objects.

Our **perceptions** impact our emotions, causing happiness or worries, which contribute towards building our goals & objectives, and the will to achieve the goals or meet the objectives. At the end of this chain - a massive, intangible, complex chain - lies the manifestation of it all, namely the satisfaction and / or the payback (or its lack thereof). And the satisfaction (or dis-satisfaction) that we feel will lead on to prayers whose extent is determined by the gap between the ideal and the real!

If we pause to reflect even for a brief minute or two, we will find that it is this complex chain that is at the root of every action we have taken, every bit of pain or happiness that we experienced, every moment of truth that flashed before us, taking cues from who we are, and in turn redefining us, a continuous process that never stops. Yes, it is a self-fulfilling cycle that feeds and replenishes itself, contributing to its own momentum, but also slowing it down, spinning off outcomes on its tangents.

We think, therefore we are and continue to be. It is how we know we exist. It is how we thrive in the universe. It is what makes the universe work.

Research has shown that you're what you believe yourself to be. The thought is the basic defining element driving our existence, moving us in directions known and unknown, in consonance or dissonance with the universe, creating the state of happiness and satisfaction, or sadness and frustration, and influencing the course of actions that consist our lives. Clear & definite desire is the only foundation for a great destiny,

"You are what your deep, driving desire is
As your desire is, so is your will
As your will is, so is your deed
As your deed is, so is your destiny"

– Brihadaranyaka Upanishad

And this gives all of us the ideal handle to achieve peace and happiness. The beauty is that our mind is under our control.

Be the master of your own minds. And in this thought lies the keys that could help us to unravel the secret to realizing who we really are, which in turn helps us to understand why we do what we do! It is easy to come across people who may break into acts of reverence when passing by a place of worship, and there may be others who may not notice the fact that they're passing by such a place. Whist this could be a very unconscious act on part of these people, we fail to notice that these seemingly random and unconscious actions could have been driven by **innate beliefs** that are ingrained into our sub-conscious or driven by learnings that grow out of experiences, which get stored away deep within, triggering actions that are unconscious. There are several such actions that we undertake in our everyday existence for which we do not have a trace of origin, nor a track of behaviours. But, still, they end up defining us in many ways unknown to us.

"One who has control over the mind is tranquil in heat and cold, in pleasure and pain, and in honour and dishonour; and is ever steadfast with the Supreme Self."

– The Bhagavad Gita

When we become more aware of the core thoughts that drive the inner attitudes of our minds, we also get hold of the levers that we can push or pull to change the external life. If we let negative thoughts take over our minds, we may feel unhappy, depressed and miserable. If we feed the minds with positive thoughts, we become happy, and fulfilled. The journey from unhappy to happy does not lie outside ourselves, but well within us and in our grasp, though getting to it is not without some effort.

Yes, it is not an insurmountable mountain, even as it may seem one at the outset, when we look at it through the prism of a current state of existence. The key to **unlock** the gates to this journey, lies in our ability to uncover the thoughts driving our actions, which gives us the ability to make the right changes. But in order to get to this state, the most important means also lies in the realm of our own thoughts – which is our belief in our own selves. Belief leads to conviction and conviction leads to clarity of thoughts, which in turn drive concerted actions that are at the forefront of building up towards the desired outcomes. Our desires, hence, hinge on our ability to believe in our selves, and not on the universe around us. In fact it is the thoughts within us that shape our existence in relation to the universe, and not the other way round as we are led to widely believe.

The Ultimate Truth of Transformation!

You can't change the Shadow until you
change the Object

Nothing will change until you change within!

Your external world is nothing but the exact
reflection of your inner-world!!

The Ultimate Truth of Transformation!

– His Holiness Shri Aasaanji

www.atmayoga.in

THE SHAPE OF THOUGHTS – THE GOOD, THE BAD, THE POSITIVE, THE NEGATIVE

Consciousness - The power behind all powers!

Every human being is blessed with the ability to make the conscious connection with the consciousness which you call as the oneness with the divine in meditation!

The ultimate truth of meditation is to experience the conscious connection with the consciousness,

This is the power behind every power!

– His Holiness Shri Aasaanji

We have seen how thoughts form the basis of our existence and define us in many ways. Such is the power of thought that they don't just define the existence, but also embody the selves, and are the prime movers of every action voluntary or involuntary. We are, at any moment of our existence, determined only by the thought that the mind holds at the moment and the way it courses through us and manifests as us, in the universe. From desire to dedication to despondency to dejection to delirium, or ambition to attachment to achievement to austerity, thoughts that course through our beings are very diverse and take several different shapes and forms. These thoughts conscious or unconscious, end up defining us either momentarily or for significant lengths of time, orchestrating the being and determining the manifestation of our selves in the universe at any point in time.

Our thoughts have various **attributes**, take on different colours and forms and have a powerful and a very direct impact on our body, our appearance and our movements. And it is these attributes that come together in different ways to give a distinct shape to the thought, which in turn is an inherent part of how we manifest in the universe at a particular moment in our existence. We could be the manifestation of a thought, or a combination of thoughts, or a stream of thoughts with some dominating. This manifestation can either elevate or degrade one's existence, only by virtue of what the mind is carrying inside it at that moment. Whether serene and austere or animated and rigorous, it is the thought that provides the shape, form or colour that manifests on the self.

"The one who controls his senses by the mind, and without attachment, engages the organs of action in the performance of prescribed duties, is said to be of steady intelligence"

– The Bhagavad Gita

We are led to believe and contend that our key manifestation in this universe is the physical self. We are judged, appreciated, and comprehended by this manifestation. If we take a step backward, and introspect and reflect on what is giving shape to this self, we will realize the power of the thought driving the existence. Our perception of the self and the universe will begin changing when we reimagine this construct of the self. If we pause for a moment to imagine thoughts as things, and the self as the container of these things, it will instantly become clear to us that the self is merely a form that is dictated and shaped by the thought.

Imagine yourself at different circumstances in your day or in your life. Think of the moment when something did not progress as expected or when you realized that you made a mistake, one which has a negative impact on your present state. Perhaps if you stood in front of a mirror at that moment, it is easy to observe that the physical appearance is starkly different from the moment when you were ebullient and joyful owing to a positive event which may be the outcome of a concerted and focused effort. Just how is it possible that the same physical being could appear so different at different instances, purely on the weight of the thought that is coursing through the mind of the being. But such is the impact of our thoughts that they end up manifesting in ways that we do not realize, unconsciously shaping our existence momentarily and in turn impacting our relationship with the universe around us.

The universe around us mirrors our existence and beams it back to us either reinforcing or rejecting our actions, and this in turn leads on to the next train of thoughts and their manifestations or actions, thus leading to the cycle of manifestations that are self-reinforcing and end up as a positive spiral or a negative one. And such a spiral, if it holds sway over a length of time, could play a significant role in the shaping the manifestations permanently.

The shape of thoughts is well understood by likening it to a river. It originates in the cool and pleasant mountain climes as a mild stream, gentle and beautiful, lively and pleasant, patient but never lethargic. As it progresses, and encounters a rock, it tries to change course, meandering and wavering momentarily, but hewing a new path and an existence. And then comes a steep fall, and it has to take the plunge, pushing objects away by force, breaking new ground, sometimes painfully, but progressing nevertheless.

By the time it reaches the plains, it takes the shape of a know-it-all, with the arrogant but confident appearance of having been there and done that, a benign and a peaceful existence at most times, but capable of turning into a raging torrent, impatient to get through, bearing a visage of the destructor. However, for all this rage and show of power, as it nears the end of its existence, before shedding its identity and becoming one with a universal entity, it is a benevolent force once again, shedding all pretences even to the extent of being helpless, as if in deep contemplation about the path that it took and how it coursed through.

As a river is a gurgling stream once, a gentle brook the other, a raging waterfall the next, and a vast, peaceful expanse at another instance, so too does the self take various shapes and forms in the course of its journey through the universe, in its incessant quest to find its own nook, to become one with the universe, and achieve the next stage in the path of existence.

Whether momentarily in response to stimuli that we receive, or as an outcome of the broader set of influences around us, our thoughts are constantly influenced, challenged, modified and disrupted in many myriad ways. These, impacts on our thoughts, in turn take on shapes and colours as they manifest within and to the outside world in many different ways making us who we are in the context of this universe.

The power to achieve inner peace depends on the ability to exercise the power of understanding and appreciating the thought that courses through the being at every moment, and achieving a control over it, much as a river's energy is channelled into useful purposes by way of canals and dams. The power to control and regulate the flow of thoughts, gives us the power to build our existence and construct our destiny, one thought at a time. Each thought that manifests our existence has a consequence and gives it a shape, much as the river is shaped by the forces around it.

Good begets the good and bad begets the bad. Love brings forth love, and hate mirrors itself similarly. A positive thought has a beneficial impact on the existence, whereas a negative one delivers a destructive impact.

Such is the **consequence** of thought, inescapable in its manifestation and profound in impact.

Thoughts do not occur one at a time, but like the staccato burst of a machine gun sometimes or the sweet cacophony of the morning birds at other times, hitting all at once, competing for **attention**, trying to overpower one another in a fierce fight to manifest the being. It is of paramount importance to separate the wheat from the chaff, so that we consciously avoid the ones that manifest as an undesirable shape on the existence.

Achieving control over the thoughts is not the most important endeavour. The most important endeavour is to determine which thoughts deserve attention, and single them out for action. Positive or negative; good or bad; it lies in this ability to stem the torrential flow of thoughts, and channel the right ones; to map the cacophony of sounds, and pick out the ones that are musical to the existence. Learning to identify and cherish the right thoughts will enrich and turn the existence into a rewarding one for the individual and the universe.

No dream, no goal, no objective is difficult to achieve, if we achieve the power to identify the right set of thoughts to shape our existence. The ability to get to this is just a result of how much we are engaged within ourselves, with our thoughts, and fortified by the awareness of the influences that are shaping these thoughts. Establishing a conscious connect with our thoughts is the most powerful means of shaping ourselves and manifesting our strengths.

The Mind is like a Mirror !

The positive image you hold in your mind is the highest source to bring the positive change you want in your life

The divine truth is, what you have in life is what you have in mind

– His Holiness Shri Aasaanji

www.atmayoga.in

MANIFESTATION OF THOUGHTS – PHYSICAL, BEHAVIOURAL, ATTITUDINAL

Change your Karma To Change your Life !!

Every human being is blessed with the power to change their life only when they realize the truth about Karma!

Once understood, every situation is reversible…

Even the irreversible is reversible!

The one and only way to change your life is to change your karma..

And the only way to change your karma is to practice meditation!

This is the untold truth about success!

– His Holiness Shri Aasaanji

We know that thoughts define our existence. And that these thoughts also take on various shapes and forms as they course through the beings, impacted by the universe. It is this nature of our thoughts that puts them at the centre of our existence. And it is thus, by virtue of the myriad thoughts that exist within us, that who we are is nothing but a manifestation of the thoughts that the mind holds. This realization is key to everything that we indulge in, because it helps us to understand the momentary manifestation and to shape this manifestation to achieve what we want to.

Manifestations, according to The Gita, are infinite, and range from that which lack a form, to that which is all pervading; from the benevolent to the destructive; and from the virtuous and tenacious to the weak and wavering.

"A happy heart enlightens the face, but a sad heart reflects a broken spirit. A discerning mind seeks knowledge, but the mouth of fools feeds on folly. The entire life of the afflicted seems disastrous, but a good heart feasts continuously."

Proverbs 15:13-15, The Holy Bible

And the key to understanding and appreciating this manifestation lies in unravelling the layers of this manifestation, which consists of three distinct planes – the physical being; the behavioural wrapper of the being; and the attitudinal aura cast by the being. It is these three layers that combine to make us who we are in each moment of existence. It is this package that constitutes who we are and, relates to and engages with the universe. And as it goes through this process, it is at once **shaping** itself as well as the universe by virtue of the continuous exchange. It is nothing but these thoughts we hold that shape, build, and power the manifestations and its interactions with the universe.

It is quite a simplistic depiction of any manifestation in this universe, but something that fails to be noted because it is quite common place. But it is exactly how we are perceived by others, that is, by the virtue of our physical manifestation, overlaid by the thoughts that drive our behaviour, which are in turn shaped further by the thoughts that consist the innate attitudes which we carry. Every person is a manifestation of an unmistakable combination of these three building blocks, constituted by thoughts at different levels, some momentary and transient, while some are deeper and more pervasive.

"Your world is shaped by your own thoughts
What a person thinks is what he becomes"

– Maitri Upanishad

However, these are just **building blocks** and we have to realize that we carry several such blocks within us, thoughts that is, which we use to construct and reconstruct ourselves in many different ways, as we go about engaging with the universe around us. The same individual - eg a man – is at once a father, a husband, a son, a professional – perhaps, an employee or an employer, a constituent of the civic community, and possibly many other manifestations, as determined by the thoughts that constitute his mind, which come together at different times to depict such manifestations. Each of these are structures that are constructed from building blocks of the same kind – our physical, behavioural and attitudinal manifestations.

The structures stay with us, rarely modified and / or reconstructed, but never demolished. And, mostly we do not deconstruct, thus carrying them around with us like shells, as does the tortoise. Just like how a tortoise carries around its sanctuary on its back, so too do we use these shells that we construct as our own sanctuaries, trying to block out thoughts and inputs that we may deem inimical to the building blocks that we have used to build our shells.

A pertinent question to ask ourselves is, "are these protective shells or burdens that we carry around?". Does the shell shield the tortoise from evils and dangers, or is it also a burden that slows it down, and prevents its progress in evolution ?

The Galapagos tortoises discovered by Charles Darwin are an evolutionary marvel. Giant sized, and slow moving, they managed to cross the oceans and reach continents far off from their traditional habitat, but this is attributed to the strength of their basic features, rather than their ability to adapt. It is seen from the fact that, though distant cousins of these tortoises were found in other continents, none of these species have managed to acquire the ability to swim, but have managed to get around by the ability to stay afloat, going without food for long durations and flowing with the tides & currents.

Perhaps the tortoise embodies this statement by the legendary comic character, Winnie the Pooh: *"Don't underestimate the value of Doing Nothing, of just going along, listening to all the things you can't hear, and not bothering."*

It has two different messages, if we try to expand this metaphor of the tortoise into the realm of manifestations – one could stay simple and humble, and manage to be happy and peaceful, but not fight for evolution; or one could constantly pick up newer thoughts and evolve, gain the ability to manifest in different ways, but only if there's a clear realization of what we are constructing and if there is a need to deconstruct.

A student heading into an examination, very well prepared, having read through all of the text, practiced enough, and eager to test oneself, is always a picture of confidence; a smile on the lips, gentle calmness on the face, a steady and assured gait and a firm, unruffled resolve. The resolute calmness is a manifestation of the mind's focus on the tasks at hand, and the confidence that springs from the solid preparation and effort. The everyday existence is akin to examination of sorts consisting of several tests, small and large, constantly challenging us to manifest ourselves in the best of forms, and the ways we respond is directed by the thoughts shaping the manifestations. It is the clarity of thoughts that we carry within, that enables us to get the best out of all situations.

The thoughts that we hold in our mind have the power to shape our appearance. "An upright and an open stance, with shoulders spread wide, a straight gaze, a confident gait" – this is how the revolutionary poet Subramanya Bharathi describes a confident woman. If confidence is the reflection of a prepared mind, it requires no stretch of imagination to understand that a prepared mind is one that contains purposeful thoughts, that are meant to drive the us towards the desired outcomes. Distilling the right set of thoughts provides clarity of purpose and achieving the purpose. A confident, calm and collected self is a manifestation of clear, purposeful, positive thinking, shaped by good intent and backed by an intense belief in the self .

A child goes from being cantankerous one minute to happy and pleased the next, and this 'behaviour' is generally believed to be caused by the perceived state of fulfilment that it feels. A child's sense of fulfilment is a product of its instantaneous wants and desires, as it does not have the capability to look beyond the instant, living in that instant, devoid of beliefs, or expectations, or fears or responsibilities; the typical thoughts that make or mar anyone's day or even a particular moment, and shape the behaviour at that moment or day or any particular period in time. That is right. It is these beliefs, preferences, opinions, desires, hopes, fears, prejudices, and such, that course through the mind constantly, that end up playing a significant role in shaping our dispositions and hence our behaviours at various points in time.

And so, typically, one who is not cognizant of the thoughts driving behaviours, will end up displaying different dispositions at different instances. However, someone who is in good command of these thoughts will be seen displaying a more predictable and standard disposition, thus reducing the frictions with the universe and paving the path for a more smoother progression in life and fortunes. A child always knows the reason driving his / her behaviour and it is momentary and it is driven by a clear, unambiguous goal. The question to ask is "do I know, why I'm behaving in this manner, in this moment ?" What matters is, whether we are in the moment, or if we're driven by a past occurrence or a future possibility.

The third dimension of manifestation is the attitude underpinning the behavioural and physical manifestations. Much like our behaviours, our attitudes are shaped through our life experiences, good or bad, but are also manifestations of how the experiences shape our thinking. An individual may not act in the same manner, at all points in time, in response to the same stimulus. This response is shaped by the attitudinal manifestation of the thoughts.

Much unlike a child, as we grow in life, we tend to carry thoughts over a long period of time, sometimes incubating and evolving them, sometimes trying to uncover layers for clarity, sometimes as memories and feelings, and many a time as desires, expectations, and the fears and insecurities thereof. It is paramount that we understand the role that our thoughts play in manifesting us in this universe, and work to delineate and segregate them, according to their relevance to the moment.

Your life is not pre-determined, you create your future!!

The simple fact of life is that your life is pre-destined, but not pre-determined,

And, To change your life, you need to change your karma;

Your karma cannot be changed by anyone other than by your own self!

Your fate is your decision, your life is your own creation

– His Holiness Shri Aasaanji

A living embodiment of spiritual knowledge and healing power, Guruji makes us realise that every human being is a gift of God with incredible self-healing power, and, is a positive change agent to create a better future with peace, brother hood and harmony. He makes us aware that in God's creation there is no discrimination and always draws attention to the fact that the Supreme Power is one and same for everyone and that we all belong to One Human Family.

www.atmayoga.in

HAPPINESS – A STATE OF THE BODY & MIND

Happiness - The Essence of Success !

Success is not the only way to happiness,
Happiness is the seed to success...
Life will be full of happening when you realize that
happiness is just a beginning!
Intelligent people will do everything for happiness,
But spiritual people will do everything happily !
Its highly difficult to find happiness within
but its highly impossible to find anywhere else

– His Holiness Shri Aasaanji

Happiness – a term that evokes several different feelings, memories, emotions, physical and other manifestations. It is a term that can mean many different things to each of a group of individuals who are similar or alike in nature and could be observing the same event or occurrence and/or experiencing the same outcome – that is, even for people who are very similar to each other, the same experience may evoke different thoughts, feelings and emotions.

We are happy for ourselves, for our friends, relatives, or families; we're happy for our nations, our communities, our favourite sports teams or rock bands, and for several different, broader purposes. We're happy when we start something or when we finish something; when we get something or when we give away something. We're happy when we do something, or when we are idle, doing nothing.

Happiness is so intrinsically mixed up with the nature of human existence that the term finds a place even in a document as specific and unique as the Declaration of Independence, considered as one of the foundations of the constitution and governance in the USA. The declaration enshrines happiness as a fundamental right when it states, "….certain unalienable Rights, that among these are Life, Liberty and the pursuit of Happiness".

Happiness is a universal goal of existence, something that the universe strives to achieve, while constantly trying to grapple with the mystery of what it is - whether it is an emotion or a thought or a physical experience. Is it a mere smile on the lips or a rapturous state of the body or ecstasy of the mind, or is it all of this at the same time. How do we understand happiness, and moreover, is it essential to understand happiness to achieve that state, or is it a product of our thoughts and actions, and something that is not to be pursued explicitly, as propounded by Buddha :

"A guarded and a tamed mind does not get attached to nor tend to focus on whatever it comes across; A mind so tamed and guarded brings happiness"

– Dhammapada

Research indicates that one of the factors that determine happiness is inherited – the inheritance of the genetic mix that play a role in our physical and/or mental states, and the inheritance of circumstances such as financial and social positions, the worldly possessions and such material riches which undoubtedly play a role in self-perception as well as how we are perceived by others.

However, does this account for all the factors responsible for delivering the state of happiness. If so, will it not be universally acclaimed that physical possessions (including genetic inheritances) determine happiness? Whilst inheritances govern or influence the physical state of being and existence, they, by no means, exercise control over the mind and the inner-self which is governed by the mind, and the thoughts that it carries. Unless, of course, the quest for happiness is driven only by the quest for achievement of desires.

One of the greatest philosophers known to mankind, Aristotle, stated thus : *"Happiness depends on ourselves"*. It is not something that is ready made but comes from our own actions, and how we manage our desires. This is also indicated in the Bhagavad Gita which says *"He attains peace into whom all desires enter as waters enter the ocean, which when filled from all sides, remains unmoved; but not the man who is full of desires"*.

Are these observations, coming from such stalwarts, in stark contrast to what science has discovered, that happiness is also genetic and circumstantial? On the contrary, in fact, even the scientific approaches, to understand the basis of happiness, have come to the same conclusion that the every day activities and actions have a nearly 40% impact on the state of happiness!

Happiness is not something that is completely wired into our existence from the beginning, but is a constantly evolving phenomenon as we move forth in our lives. Neither is it a reality that happiness is the outcome of a consistently positive emotional state in which we chose to ignore anything that causes despair, and maintain a constant state of feeling joy or cheerfulness at all times.

Happiness, rather, is the ability to understand that life is not a product of our manifestations, but also the product of its interactions with other manifestations that influence, impact, and disrupt at time. Many a time, it is not in our power to bring about changes and modifications in other manifestations, but is well within our abilities to accept these influences, impacts, and disruptions, internalize these appropriately and respond peacefully. It then becomes quite clear that happiness is just not about staying positive in the face of any situation, but rather face and accept the negative and then build within ourselves the skills and abilities to manage the negative experiences better.

If there is one aspect about which all the scriptures and philosophical schools of thought agree universally, it is this that the constant pursuit of worldly desires lead to a state of **discontentment**, disillusionment and hence a state of un-happiness. It has been widely postulated that the key to unlocking the treasure trove of happiness lies in :

- a steady pursuit of knowledge, or

- an unwavering commitment to performing one's duties irrespective of outcomes, or

- mastery over the senses, and,

a dedication to meditating on the self, which helps to still the mind and ensure serenity, while also helping to uncover the deepest fears and confront them, to pave a better path towards the future.

As goes an ancient Chinese proverb, *"If you want happiness for a lifetime - help someone else"*, which is further reinforced by the philosopher Lao Tzu, *"Be content with what you have; rejoice in the way things are. When you realize there is nothing lacking, the world belongs to you."*

A very common and an old adage that most people would have carried with them from childhood is, "A sound mind in a sound body". A state of happiness is not a possibility unless the physical and spiritual manifestations are in synchronization with each other and complement each other well. A disoriented physical manifestation cannot be the container of a still and serene spirit; while a disoriented spirit will not allow the existence of a strong and steady physical manifestation. It is a symbiotic relationship between body and mind, each complementing the other, co-existing, and fostering each other, enabling the elevation of existence or its depravity thereof.

Feeling joyful has its health perks as well. A growing body of research also suggests that happiness can improve physical health; feelings of positivity and fulfilment seem to benefit cardiovascular health, the immune system, inflammation levels, and blood pressure, among other things. Happiness has even been linked to a longer lifespan as well as a higher quality of life and well-being.

Our thoughts influence our perceptions, which, in turn, lead to formation of our beliefs. It should, hence, be borne in the mind that If we let negative thoughts fill and take over the mind, it has an impact on our perceptions, both of the self and the external world, which could lead us into a state of discontentment or disorientation, leaving us feeling unhappy, depressed and miserable. If we feed our mind with positive thoughts and perceptions, we will instantly find our selves being freed of burdens and the universe appearing to be a beautiful and a friendly place, leading us into states of hope rather than despair, resulting in a happy frame of mind.

"The good (**SHREYAS**) and the pleasant (**PREYAS**) come to a man and the thoughtful mind turns around them and distinguishes. The wise choose out the good from the pleasant, but the dull soul chooses the pleasant (**PREYAS**) rather than the getting of his good (**SHREYAS**) and its having."

– Kathopanishad (1.2.2)

The beauty is that our mind is under our control. We can be the master of our own minds. And, when we use this mastery to drive a positive thinking, it inevitably results in a positive impact on our physical states, manifesting in terms of steady breathing, smooth flow of blood and an overall elevated sense of preparedness to engage with the universe around us, rather than encounter it and react to it. As Gita says, a prepared mind and body, which is driven only by clear commitment to a deed, rather than the outcome, is better positioned to achieve results and move on.

We are habituated to think that we will be happy once we get to a certain milestone or achieve a certain goal. However, being the great adapter that humans are, we will quickly baseline this new state and start seeking the next goal or milestone, taking us back to the earlier state of mind, longing for happiness. Goals and milestones are not the **markers of happiness**, but indicate progress on specific scales. The key is to not get carried away for such scales of measures, and trap ourselves in vicious circles, that are merely illusory by their nature and not permanent.

There are certain aspects in life that do not have any direct connection to a measuring scale of any kind – money, position, award, strength, etc. Some of those include: the ability to broaden our mind through knowledge, perform tasks to the best of our abilities, maintain equanimity, love others as we love ourselves, show kindness and compassion, display gratitude, live in the present, live without grudges, celebrate oneself through exercise and grooming, and a host of such intangible items. None of these are specific to our ability to possess any kind of material content, nor can be measured by any specific yardstick, but it is a state of existence that is enabled by a set of beliefs and values.

We can get to this state by immensely concentrating on what we want to become. Such an exercise drives us towards building an image of what we want to be, where we want to get to, making it appear closer, and taking away the anxiety borne out of our innate fears and insecurities. A mind that is able to achieve this state finds itself in an elevated state of happiness due to the clarity found in the journey and its destination. But the concentration needs the practice. Eventually, that practice will lead to subconscious actions, automatically giving priority to the positive thoughts and feelings. And that will deliver a tremendous power to achieve the goals, no matter how difficult they are perceived to be.

Love is not everything, but, everything is love....

Not how much you love others,
How much you love your own self
determines happiness!
We can only share what we have....
so always practice self-love!

Love yourself first. Focus on your future, and do not compromise for others. Never compare yourself, but listen to your inner voice. This will make life greater than what you think.

– His Holiness Shri Aasaanji

www.atmayoga.in

THOUGHTS – FLOW OF ENERGY

You are God!!

You are not the mind.....

You are not the body....

You are the non-physical invisible infinite power, gifted with a physical body,

To experience oneness with the formless ultimate power!

That which created this universe is right now existing within you as Life Energy!!

– His Holiness Shri Aasaanji

Thoughts, these have been in our thoughts!! What do we do without those!! They embody us, are the proof that we exist, and manifest us in many different ways. We looked at several metaphors about thoughts – flowing water that pushes through nature, fills up vast expanses, enriches, quenches, powers, and eventually reigns over everything.

Water, an omnipresent visible and a tangible manifestation of nature is something that instantly elicits several different images – the powerfully flowing river, the calm ponds & lakes, the dull and dirty wastewater. We instantly associate all these with energy, or water happens to be the force of nature that we can see, hear, touch and feel, an embodiment of the power of this universe. This **embodiment** is perceived as the manifestation of energy present in universe.

We look at someone and comment that they're radiant and bright, or, alternatively, dull and morose. We look at children and comment about their exuberance. We look at a marathon runner and wonder about the endurance. What is it about these people that makes us perceive them in this manner. Is it a physical attribute?

Radiance, brightness, calm & serene, dullness, morose, exuberance, endurance – are these mere descriptions of physical appearance and attributes? If these are mere physical appearances, is it not something that anyone can achieve? Is it just about keeping good health, so that you are strong, active, capable of moving about smoothly and without assistance? Or is it about achieving a flawless complexion and dressing up well. If this were the case, will all these attributes not be things that could be bought and installed?

We look at water and perceive it in several different forms, purely based on its appearance at its moment of manifestation. We may perceive it in many ways, but that does not change the fact that it is the same water – H_2O!! Our perception does not reflect any change to the fundamental content of water, but its appearance which it exudes by virtue of the energy that it contains in the moment. It is this energy that makes us perceive water in many different ways, stillness to exuberant, and pure to dirty.

Such is the nature of energy within, that it manifests itself in many different shapes and appearances, while not changing the fundamental form. Just as water is animated by the forces of nature in this universe, we are animated by the thoughts that course through us in the moment. A child is the best example of the way thoughts manifest in the form of energy, taking on a variety of appearances reflecting its innate thoughts. The child when it is well rested and fed, is what we usually refer to as a 'bundle of energy', jumping, running bouncing, playing without a care in the world about what else is happening around it. Just like Newton's 3rd law of motion, the child continues in this state until acted upon by another force called hunger and / or sleep!! Imagine this same child if it is deprived of food or if it is craving a toy, and this bundle of energy is suddenly a source of disruption. This is the purest and simplest possible manifestation of thoughts into energy.

And this is what the Shiva Sutra refers to as "Nartaka atma : The dancer is Self "; the stage is the inner self. The spectators are the organs of senses and it is a theory that finds resonance elsewhere too:

"As someone thinks within himself, so he is"

– Proverbs 23:7, The Holy Bible

As we move ahead in life, we grow beyond needs that are simple and immediate, and add more by way of responsibilities, cares, demands on us, and plans for the future, both short and long. Every waking moment is a manifestation of a complex mix of several such thoughts, which pervade the mind all the time, and also manifest during sleep, as dreams. And just as a fed and satisfied child is a bundle of energy, a mind full of thoughts has its own manifestation in terms of the energy that we exude.

You're watching someone bullying people. Suddenly, you find yourself almost taking a step back, and you feel disturbed. It's almost as though the person is throwing something at you. What you're experiencing is the toxic energy from that person's thoughts—and it's real. Mental energy sucks others in. Think of hanging out with someone who's constantly depressed or negative and how you feel around them. Fear breeds fear. The fearful mind generates fearful probabilities. The depressed mind generates depressing possibilities. But the same can be said for the positive. The excited mind generates exciting possibilities. The joyful mind generates joyful possibilities. And the list goes on. We are what we think, and what we think about most will grow.

"It is our own mental attitude which makes the world what it is for us. Our thoughts make things beautiful; our thoughts make things ugly. The whole world is in our own minds. Learn to see things in the proper light"

– Swami Vivekananda

What we're doing with our minds, our words, our attitudes, and our beliefs affects the people around us. What if someone were to tell us that there's a black cloud hanging over us and it's affecting them? Or that we're creating a toxic work environment by letting our stress affect everyone in the office? There's real energy being emitted from our thoughts and affecting others.

Water is pure, calm and serene when it is still and carries no impurities; exuberant and joyful when propelled through its course by nature's force; at times angry and destructive when its natural course is impeded by other forces, and is unclean and dirty when it allows impurities to enter into its being. And it is just as so with us, in that our appearances are nothing but the reflection of the thoughts that are encapsulated inside our minds. The energy that our appearance exudes, be it exuberance or sloth, is an indication of what courses through our minds at that point.

If we chose to pause for a brief moment, stop all actions, and try to slow down the flow of thoughts in the mind, it will instantly become apparent to us, what is flowing through the mind, and in turn how it is manifesting in the flow of energy in our physical appearance. If we are able to unravel the multiple threads, separate and segregate them, we give ourselves the power to decide which is the thought that should manifest the being in the moment.

Every minute of every day, the body is physically reacting, literally changing, in response to the thoughts that run through the mind. And these thoughts are triggered by several stimuli all around us, most of which we don't even realise consciously. However, once seeded, these thoughts germinate and grow into many different shapes and forms, and it's a very complex process that we fail to figure out how it when was each thought seeded and shaped. It's not easy (but not impossible) to trace the path taken. "That's a little like asking where the forest begins. Is it with the first leaf, or the tip of the first root?" says Charles Jennings, director of neurotechnology, at the MIT institute of brain research. The brain is such a massive activity centre, receiving and transmitting several millions of signals every second, that it's like a layperson trying to take-in with bare eyes, the workings of a modern car driven by several electronic circuits, all functioning together in sync. While this task is possible with a computer, brain imaging tools are still in their infancy!! Researchers are hoping, someday, to be able to identify the parts of brains fired by different impulses, physical and emotional.

What flows through the mind also sculpts the brain in permanent ways. Think of the mind as the movement of information through the nervous system, which on a physical level is all the electrical signals running back and forth, most of which is happening below conscious awareness.

A marathon runner exudes a lot of energy because the mind is solely focused on the path and puts the entire focus on the feet, the rhythm with which they move and the breath that drives this rhythm. It brings a calmness akin to meditation, instantly manifesting as a calm determination. A student going to an examination, having put in the right preparation, unmindful of the consequences of the outcome, will be a picture of calm determination.

Low mental energy can easily translate to a drop in physical energy, too. Physical movement might not involve the same level of cognition as, say, solving a math problem or preparing a report. Still, it requires brainpower. Some experts describe mental energy as a mood state where we feel productive, motivated, and prepared to get things done. A lack of mental energy, then, might mean we don't feel capable of much at all. Even when we aren't physically tired, our thoughts might drift along like a snail in slow motion.

Emotions have energy and what we focus on, we fuel. It is key to consent to our uncomfortable emotional state, then ask what we would like instead (something, of course, that we can create and maintain). Learning to release resistance increases accountability, emotional engagement and productivity. Every cell in the body is replaced about every two months. So, the good news is, we can reprogram our pessimistic cells to be more optimistic by adopting positive thinking practices, like mindfulness and gratitude, for permanent results

A manifestation of calmness and determination exudes positivity, which is reflected back to the self by the entire universe. It is also perceived as positive thinking. It comes from telling the mind that that the immediate situation is not the final destination, but a step in the process, a cog in the wheel, which needs to be handled with skill, but not to be overwhelmed by the anxiety about the final outcome. This is the key to harnessing the power of the universe, and driving positive energy into our actions.

Self-realization is nothing but realizing that
the power within you is

the same power which has created the entire
universe;

the power that we refer to as God;

And some people mention it as The divine,
The Ultimate,

The Cosmic Energy, but in reality all remains
the same!

– His Holiness, Shri Aasaanji

BREAK THE SHACKLES – *TACKLE FEAR AND SELF DOUBT*

You are More Powerful than You Think !

When you blame,

You accept that you are powerless and settle with the pain...

But in reality no matter how bad the situation is,

The present situation is not your final destination!

Every human being is blessed with the power to rise above any situation!

Get ready to raise again

– His Holiness Shri Aasaanji

The mind is a **container**. It contains thoughts that are centred on principles, relationships, knowledge, actions, happiness, desires, attractions, distractions, dislikes, discontentment, fears and insecurities. The mind is not a defined organ with a shape or a form, and it takes on the shapes and forms of the thoughts that it contains, and the thoughts that dominate its space. It is an inherent part of us, lurking behind an unknown curtain, and yet goading, prodding, driving us, to listen, tune-in, imbibe the environment around us, and react. It is the unseen, unknown force which drives our neural system to respond to stimulus perceived by the senses.

It is like a deep well where dwell fishes, insects, and reptiles, and plants and algae and several life forms, and rocks and mud. It is hard to look at the surface and get an idea of what it contains. The drop of a bucket into the depths is enough to disturb this surface and bring to the fore a variety of shapes and forms, which may have been lurking beneath the surface unknown hitherto. The key determinant of success here is the ability to draw a clear bucketful of water devoid of dirt and debris. It may seem quite complex, and yet is an action that is undertaken routinely, unconsciously, purely by virtue of the forces of habit, and by everyday people who are not aware when they undertake a task.

"Captivity in Maya and liberation from it is determined by the mind. If it is attached to the world, one is in bondage, and if the mind is detached from the world, one gets liberated."

– The Bhagavad Gita

It is critical to understand that an engaged mind is the key to liberation, and to prevent the blockades of bondage. An engaged mind is one that is capable of differentiating the various sensory stimulus that give rise to the thoughts, which then have the potential to drive actions. The engaged mind is one that is in conversation with itself and is able to clearly delineate the thoughts dwelling within itself. It is thus able to compartmentalize and focus on the needful at the moment.

Mere seeing is of no value if the mind is not absorbing the sight and imbibing the right detail that are relevant to our functioning and our existence. A music that could otherwise be soothing or enjoyable could be lost on the ears, if the mind is pre-occupied and is not tuned into the sense. This is not a limitation of the sense (not to consider specific physical disabilities like impaired vision or hearing), however it is a limitation of the mind that is not registering the input coming in from the senses.

A mind that is not picking out the right details from the stimuli, and processing it for the necessary information, is a mind that is overwhelmed with all that it contains, which too is clearly all over the place as well. Such a mind has no way of figuring out how to handle the newer inputs. Its akin to a storage space where objects or things are not stacked or arranged in a particular manner, and so you do not have the ability to utilize the space in a wise manner. Imagine being in a hurry to get somewhere and planning on a specific attire that we know that we have, but however finding it hard to locate it in the storage space. Imagine its impact on many other aspects of day's plan – we may slip up on the timelines, probably make someone wait unnecessarily, and imagine the impact of all this on the self, on our behaviour, our ability to act, and our outlook at that point of time.

So is the case with the mind where the thoughts are all over the place, that one does not realize which deserves attention, which is to be prioritized and acted or which is the major question be addressed at any point in time. And it seriously impairs the ability to act effectively, be decisive, coordinated, and well thought out.

And how does this manifest ?

It is that instance when we feel that nothing is working, everything is going wrong, and the whole world is stacked up against us, preventing us from reaching our objectives, blocking the path leading to our goals, lowering our self-esteem and our confidence levels. It makes us think that we're not capable enough and lack in some manner.

Is that really the case here ?

We sleep and we dream, and in the dreams we see and we hear and we smell and indulge in actions. Now, how is this possible that we see when the eyes are closed, or taste when we're not actually eating? Dreams are caused by the thoughts contained by the mind, getting triggered unconsciously and making us feel that we're going through the experiences, even as the senses are not alive. Such is the power of the mind.

However, very often we find ourselves blockaded out of the ability to process outcomes even while fully conscious. It is something that we commonly refer to as a mental block or barriers to leveraging the mind in its most powerful form. There are several aspects that give rise to these barriers, many of which are typically common to most of us, though there could also be issues and challenges that are unique for a very few. Fear, self-doubt, a general lack of confidence, inertia to step outside a comfort zone, could all be typical barriers that are faced by people commonly. A lot of these are part of beliefs that may have crept into the mind along the way, giving rise to assumptions that we make about ourselves, and push us into a self reinforcing spiral that could tend to heighten these barriers, making them seem insurmountable and leading us to despair and states that are referred to as depression.

An easier example to relate to is the case of physical health; weight loss. Several people go through the typical spiral of weight gain and the seemingly insurmountable challenge of weight loss and return to shape. Even for a person conscious of maintaining a healthy body, and who looks into all its attendant aspects like diets and exercise regimens, a brief slip-up is all that is required to tip the balance of self belief. A brief interlude, like a party, can result in an eating binge which can lead to a sudden change in the state of the body and act as a dampener on the physical activity that is to follow. While all it takes to get back on track is a simple belief in the regimen, a minor re-calibration of diets and a one-time intensification of the exercise regimen, reality is always different. It is very rare to find a person who does not know of someone or the other who may have suddenly lost belief in their well cultivated fitness regime and gone off track as to completely lose belief in oneself and one's own efforts. Where exactly did things go wrong ? Is it in the one-time indiscretion that led to the disruption of the diet program, or the loss of belief in the regimen or in the lack of courage to pull back on track, or the loss of confidence in oneself to overcome the predicament caused by very small deviation from a well laid out path.

This is just an indicative sample of how things could get out of hand. "Understand that mood follows action. The way to change your mental and physical state is to take the action first, not wait for your emotional state to change first."

The mind is so powerful that there are no limits there, and is the engine to drive you in the right direction. It is the platform for transformation that can move mountains if the right changes are made. It is not the mind that stops or limits one from getting something, or achieving a goal. It is what we do with our mind, when we do not understand what it contains and fail to notice the clutter.

The key to unravelling the tangle and charting a clear course, is to engage the mind. Just as we collect objects out of curiosity or want or greed, so too we accumulate thoughts inside the mind. A deep engagement with the mind allows us to observe the contents of this container that we call the mind, and it allows us to understand the chaos that reigns inside that space. Consistent engagement with the mind enables us to become intimately aware of what is going on in that space and what needs priority and attention and what can be pushed to the background.

Deep engagement with the mind, reorganizing the thoughts to declutter and optimizing the space by foregrounding the right thoughts and backgrounding the rest, is the surest way to unshackle the mind and allow it to regain control.

A mind that is free of shackles is a mind that is ever ready and prepared to address any challenge that confronts it. A prepared mind has the ability to conquer fear, overcome uncertainty and demolish self-doubt.

The divine truth is that

Your pain and suffering is never a part of
your destiny

But it exists because you are not taking any
self-effort to re-write your destiny

– His Holiness Shri Aasaanji

www.atmayoga.in

INNER PEACE – PATH TO POWERFUL THINKING

There is no Sustainable Success without Inner-Peace !

Inner-peace is nothing but a state of mind, free of fear, stress, anger and any form of mental disturbance....

It is the essential source to achieve success in life;.

There is no point in achieving external success by losing your inner-peace.

Success achieved by losing inner-peace can never be real success!

– His Holiness Shri Aasaanji

Happiness is an eternal quest for everyone, big or small, rich or poor, young or old. The biggest question in front of us is, whether we really know what happiness means to us ? The child seems happy when it gets its hands on the shiny new toy that it covets, only to lose this happiness when it starts coveting the next shiny item. And so is the case for everyone, with only the wants and desires being different, though the nature of thoughts is just the same.

As the 7th stanza of Adi Sankara's "Bhaja Govindam" goes:

"The childhood is lost in attachment to games. The youth is lost in attachment to woman. Old age passes with worry and anxiety, thinking over many things. But there is hardly anyone who wants to be lost (attached) in para-braman, the Supreme Spirit."

Thus, the entire lifetime is full of a wide and varied array of thoughts ranging from desires to goals to worries. We fail to realize that it is this very nature that drives us into becoming a hoarder of thoughts; result being that we end up getting lost in this miasma of thoughts and lose the idea of what it is that we really wanted, which would have made us happy.

"No temptation has overtaken you that is not common to man. God is faithful, and he will not let you be tempted beyond your ability, but with the temptation he will also provide the way of escape, that you may be able to endure it"

– 1 Corinthians 10:13, The Holy Bible

In general, peace could be referred to as the absence of violence, perhaps as preached and practiced by Mahatma Gandhi and adopted by several others who led peaceful movements across the world. Peace could also be associated with calmness, stillness, and such attributes that may be more internal to an individual. Peace in both these contexts are relevant to the achievement of happiness. As in, one's happiness is not an easy object to achieve if one is existing in the midst of a chaos, violence, and commotion. But it is not an absolute impossibility and could be achieved if one is able to transcend this situation in the mind and block out the impact of all this chaos and commotion.

It is typical of people to go on retreats, to far flung places, where nature is in abundance and human interventions are lesser, to try and experience peace. But this is based on an incorrect assumption that the driver of peace lies in the external environment. In reality what people are trying really achieve is the reduction of noise – auditory, visual, and others – which cloud the senses and stimulate thoughts that could drown the mind and send us gasping for peace.

But by mistaking this need for external quiet, what we tend to miss is the fact that it is not we who are drowning in this noise, but it is the mind. There are several different tactics that people deploy or are advised to deploy to shut out this 'noise' – take long walks, go on long breaks, listen to music, drown oneself in the lap of nature, or pick up a favourite book / story. It is common practice for corporate houses to pull away their top leaders into some remote location, so that they could put their minds to work on issues and challenges that are getting missed in the everyday 'noise'. Here again, it is clear that the aim is to block out the external noises and interruptions, so that 'peace' reigns and there is an ability to focus on a limited set of thoughts, to delve deeper or to resolve confusions.

But, is this 'peace', that is the one achieved by blocking out external 'noise' permanent, or is this a transient phenomenon, only for the chaos to return when the noise returns? There is no straightforward, universal answer to this question. Imagine a performer, a sportsperson, a rock-star, an acrobat. Could we possibly state that quiet is a very critical part of their performances ? These are people who thrive on adulation, recognition, accolades, fandom and such attributes, all of which could be termed as external noise or stimulus, and so such a noise becomes inherent to their success, which in turn determines their happiness.

Our inability to understand what is most important to us at a given point of time, is what prevents us from getting to the root of what really brings us happiness. We fail to realize that the fundamental basis of happiness is the ability to achieve peace within oneself, inner-peace, the holy grail of all spiritual pursuits. And in turn, the achievement of inner-peace is a key determinant of happiness. The two go hand – in – hand and could appear inseparable, and there is no decisive judgement yet, on which comes first – happiness or inner – peace.

The starting point of this pursuit, this journey towards happiness, this state of inner-peace, lies in unravelling the threads which make up the complex knot that we have tied up in our minds. There are always a multitude of such threads formed in the mind, in response to sensory stimulus, or as a byproduct of our longer term goals, our innate desires or even our aversions, fears, dislikes and other such emotions.

The state of unhappiness, of not being at peace, or of being in a state of constant excitement (whether positive or negative) is the result of letting several thoughts **dominate the consciousness** at the same time. It is like the cacophony in a crowded place or in a market where there are several people demanding many different things from several other people, all in a hope to address each one's particular objective.

This mirrors our existence where we let several threads of thoughts make several demands on our self all at the same time. It is like watching a favourite movie or listening to the most liked song, while also relishing your most desired dish, all at the same time. Is it realistically possible to simultaneously dwell on the joy provided by each of these experiences, and derive the maximum happiness out of these? Try as we may, it is not possible the we get the best of all these at the same time, though we may try to convince the mind that we're happy for the experiences. It is possible that we missed a pivotal moment in the movie while the mind paused momentarily to dwell on the sensation of taste or vice versa. This does not lead us into a state of happiness, rather it places us in a position of permanently seeking more and more gratification, which in turn prevents us from feeling happy, the happiness that is derived from being at peace with oneself that a particular desire or objective has been met.

We see that there are two forces at play here – one is the number of thoughts seeking to surface and manifest, and the other is the self which seeks the sense of gratification from allowing the thought to manifest and take its course. In our constant quest for the elusive inner-peace, we fail to recognize that there is a direct connection between achieving peace and gratification of the self. There are many kinds of gratifications that the self seeks – from the momentary to the everlasting. Relishing that hot cup of tea is a momentary gratification whereas ensuring that the same cup is available everyday at the same time, is an everlasting gratification.

The key to the pursuit of inner-peace is to be able to understand the sources of happiness, drive a balance between the momentary and everlasting, and ensure that the mind is filled with the right set of thoughts. It lies in the ability to foreground those thoughts that take us toward everlasting happiness. However, this does not mean that we pursue all our desires in the hope of gratifying the self. The key lies in not letting our senses drive desires, and not focusing on the materialistic aspects of life, nor indulging in negative emotions about others. If we are clear about the duties we have to perform and our skills and abilities to perform those, elevate ourselves to dedicated action without a focus on the outcomes, we allow the mind to dwell on that which is permanent, than that which is transitory. It is the process, and not the outcome that will drive us forward, hence providing an inner sense of calm by giving us a clear handle on manoeuvring our lives.

Uncluttering the mind and delineating the right set of thoughts does not alone help to achieve this state of happiness and peace. But everlasting peace comes from the recognition that the universe is the result of several manifestations, some in consonance with us and some in dissonance. All these manifestations combine to leave the universe in a constant state of evolution, and change. Our ability to achieve peace is also a product of our ability to accept change and evolve, and accept that each manifestation is as complex as ours, and are making the same attempts that we do, in their own ways.

A determined and disciplined path of meditation will take us closer to the right set of thoughts and help to unentangle the complex knots that we have created by virtue of filling the mind with thoughts that keep vying for attention, manifesting themselves and preventing a concerted course of action. The mind is the all pervading, powerful construct which provides vast possibilities that will drive us towards achieving inner-peace. Tapping its potential and unleashing its power presents us with possibilities to achieve what we want, and progress in our journey towards peace.

Peace is not the end result
But a resource one needs to possess every single
moment, for unstoppable progress;
And, It is not outside of you; It is inside you

– His Holiness Shri Aasaanji

LIVING IN THE MOMENT – THE POWER OF HERE & NOW

Make Peace with your Past to make Fortune with your Future !

Every day is a new chance and power to change your life only by realizing that you can either continue to be a prisoner of your past or the creator of your future!

In that very moment, you get the power to not just create a future, but a great fortune...

And its possible only when you decide to not to dwell in the past and let go of everything that is bothering you from the past!!

If you fail to heal the past, it will steal the peace in the present and spoil the future

– His Holiness Shri Aasaanji

Many a drop makes an ocean; thus goes an old saying, which has its equivalents in almost all languages in the world. It just goes to show how every culture thinks alike in the way the universe is perceived. We are all unified in understanding that everything that is big in this universe is nothing but an aggregation of something much smaller, and in most instances, imperceptible to the consciousness. Just like a microscope that enlarges objects and makes them visible to the naked eye, if we try and enlarge our perspectives, several minor, hitherto imperceptible details start to show themselves. We see and hear a lot, but how many details do we really notice and how many do we remember and recall.

The capabilities of the human mind are infinite, and it is capable of mapping every single detail that we want to notice and absorb. The question, hence, is about whether we chose to and how. The key to this is to enlarge our perspective of time, and chose to look at our existence as an aggregation of moments that we're living through. Every moment in this universe is a very vast container of events, thoughts and actions, few of which are immediately relevant to us whereas many are completely unrelated. Recognizing this is very critical to unleashing the power of our minds to achieve the goals and objectives that we set out for ourselves.

As we go about our everyday lives, constantly on the move, either physically or in the mind, we chose to be driven by what comes next, the next place to be or the next task to do, which is where the focus lies almost constantly. This focus on the 'next' comes at the cost of the 'now', and we fail to recognize that, driven as we are by the fear or apprehension of missing out on the 'next'. We fail to recognize that we're alive in the 'now' but are rather not at all alive to this fact and have fooled ourselves into believing that it's what comes next that is important.

How common is it for people to start a week dreaming about the week-end that comes at the end of the work week or a school week, and then get to the week-end and brood the entire week-end about the upcoming week of work or school! Or to sit at work and imagine and fantasize about a vacation, and start worrying about work piling up on the desk, while on a vacation. It is a very typical and a painfully common situation that almost everyone experiences, and lives through.

Is it not quite painful to imagine someone else going through circumstance such as this. However, are we also victims of this circumstance – engaging with thoughts that are irrelevant to the moment; being physically present in one setting, while mentally dwelling in another setting and living through all its experiences though not in a position to influence the situation or setting in any reasonable manner. Buddhism talks about what is calls the **'monkey' mind**, swinging from one thought to another, just as the monkey swings from branch to branch and tree to tree!

The monkeys keep swinging in search of a reward, something to eat or to escape from a predator or secure and safeguard themselves in some manner. And this is a very practical metaphor for what we do to ourselves as well, when we keep swinging from thought to thought, existing in a different plane than the one which we really inhabit. The mind that swings from one thought to another is a mind that is in search of a reward of some kind – an imaginary gratification that results from the imaginary existence of being at a different place at a different time.

The universal reality is that We are masters of the present, but end up being slaves of the future. If we are able to enlarge our consciousness and step down deeper into our minds, we will uncover this thrilling reality that there is a lot that we are in a position to control and drive. Very often, and for a good part of the day, we're burdened by thoughts of what happened in the past or the anxiety of what will happen in the future. And in the midst of this chaos, we do not realize that we are missing out on noticing, appreciating and focusing on the present.

Why do we have to pay attention to the present? The present which is a consequence of the past, and provides us with the best opportunity to build on something good, or effect a change and correct something that went wrong. And similarly, the present is harbinger of the future and has a major role in shaping the course of things to come. More importantly, the present is where we are situated and have the power to influence. It is most important to realize that experiencing the present moment, consciously, will ensure that the life will be lived to the fullest and will not pass by without indulging in it. So much so that, it is typical of people to start their work week thinking about the weekend that lies at the end, and then brood over the weekend thinking about all the tasks that have to be completed.

There is a lot to be had in the present – the beauty and intrigue of the task undertaken, the people who are a part of it alongside, and the very moment of executing it and the state of things around us. Every moment is an experience to be lived completely without regrets or anxiety. Dwelling in the present ensures that one does not get side-tracked by brooding about the past, nor is needlessly anxious about the future.

A ' child-like disposition' is an oft used phrase to describe a behaviour that appears to be carefree, happy and involved. And it is not without reason too. A child is unburdened by regrets, worries and anxieties, and is always in the moment, making use of what is available to stay engaged and achieve happiness. This is the disposition that we tend to lose as we grow further in life, and start carrying the burdens of expectations, which bring the twin challenges of regret about the past and an anxiety for the future.

"You neither lose any thing or gain, in this drama called life;

So stop regretting over the past and forecasting of your future, since you don't have control over the future too;

What you have in your hands is the present, so live according to Dharma and fulfil all your duties with Vairagya" .

– The Bhagavad Gita

Being in the present and living in the moment is the key to fulfilment, because when you live in the moment, your mind is uncluttered by pushing out those thoughts that drive regret or anxiety, and your focus is on where you are, what you are doing, and who is there with you in the action. Focusing on the present comes with an unexpected and a welcome gift – loss of self consciousness which is a major cause of fear, anxiety and self-doubt. When this happens, we release ourselves from the bondage of the reward – punishment trap that we set for ourselves, and open ourselves to the joy of indulging in the act, instead of watching ourselves in a detached manner, self-critiquing, finding faults with ourselves and beating ourselves up for not being good.

The power of the mind is enhanced manifold when we bring it to focus on the present, because it helps us to not only concentrate better on what we're doing, but also to ensure that the needless interference from irrelevant thoughts is minimized or avoided. By bringing our mind to bear on the immediate task or action that we're involved in we ensure that the vastness of our mind is entirely focused on the present, making it all the more easier to achieve satisfaction, which in turn feeds into the feeling of fulfilment, leads to happiness and leaves us in a better state altogether. As a by-product of this, we also get better clarity into what is it that drives our happiness, and put us on the path to success.

Success is nothing but the sense of fulfilment that we derive out of our actions. If we're able to detach ourselves from the future outcomes of the actions, as well as the factors that may or may not have led us to the present state, we leave ourselves with the thoughts concerning the present, and the immediate factors impinging the present, giving us the opportunity to have a deeper engagement with the task at hand. Being in the present, and / or living in the moment is a profound state that provides us the keys to focusing on the task at hand and not the rewards or benefits that come from completing the tasks. It is because the thought of 'reward' or 'benefit' is in itself a means of dwelling in the future, because the outcomes of the present always occur in the future. So, by dwelling in the present moment, and disregarding the thoughts associated with future, we give ourselves the power to discard our fears and insecurities, overcoming our reflexive tendencies and awakening ourselves to the most important aspects of life – engaging with the present; engaging with it in a better manner, and performing it to the fullest of our abilities.

Living in the moment is the secret to unleashing the mind to do anything to the best of our abilities, and achieving a sense of satisfaction leading to happiness.

DANGER IS REAL ! SUFFERING IS OPTIONAL !

Spiritual wisdom empowers us to be effortless in
every action, to achieve limitlessly in every aspect
and live fearlessly throughout
the life.

Every person who fears or suffers, clearly
knows what they need in the present situation,
to change the future or to face the situation when
they connect with their own-self

– His Holiness Shri Aasaanji

www.atmayoga.in

SHAPE YOUR THOUGHTS – MANAGE INTERNAL & EXTERNAL INFLUENCES

Never Give Up !

You are always bigger than the problem you face!

This is what our ancient wisdom insists; that self-realization is key to

address and easily overcome any situation!

To achieve consistent success & abundance in life, one has to

constantly remind oneself of this divine truth...

You are always bigger than the problem you face!

And then, all the failures & setbacks in life will naturally become positive feedbacks to bounce back with more success and happiness.

– His Holiness Shri Aasaanji

Aren't we all familiar with the phrase, "Faith can move mountains". What is faith ? Is it alluding to the religious beliefs that we carry within ourselves and the beliefs that we profess, which we think represents us and gives us membership to a crowd ? Or would it be something a bit more broader in definition ? It is a good question to ask ourselves.

A global pandemic that brought humanity to a stand-still almost, taking away a year or two in the lives of millions; extreme weather events attributed to human induced climate changes, and the impact of all this on the levels of compassion that we hold collectively; all this and more are enough reasons to induce a loss of faith – in religion, in people, in oneself and make us start pondering about the frailty of this human existence.

There is a lot of emphasis that we place on 'Faith', for it is a condition that does not invoke logic or reasoning. It is nearly impossible for anyone to spell out the reason for carrying a particular faith – for it defies the laws of logic and reason.

If we consider the fact that Faith is another type of thought that resides in the mind, the gravity of this phrase becomes a bit more apparent. Faith is a type of thought to which we attach a lot of power and influence. Unquestioning, firm and steady faith is capable of making us do wonderful things. It is because, such a thought tends to be all pervading in character, that it has the potential to override thoughts that could impede our abilities to achieve our goals. Faith is a powerful thought that can manifest in terms of confidence, providing a firm base for other thoughts to take root and strengthen the self.

However, we know that it is not always the case that faith leads to success. Why ? Because, it is accompanied by thoughts around who or what to put the faith on, which are not easy questions to answer, if and when they do arise. These are not easy to answer because we are part of an universe full of thoughts, including our own, and our own thoughts are influenced by several factors, both internal and external. If we take Faith as an example, it is impacted by our fears or insecurities, uncertainties, events that are unforeseen, trauma and / or setbacks and failures too. But, most importantly, it is also influenced by the forces of external opinions and advise that tend to push us into moulding our beliefs and perceptions.

Further, can Faith alone be an answer to everything? Could someone put Faith at the centre of existence and hope to reach the moon?

No, because that would turn out to be misplaced Faith. Our goals have to well aligned with our innate selves and abilities, without which Faith is of no use. The human mind is infinite and can reach out and perform anything it seeks with diligence and dedication. However, one cannot sit in prayer and meditation alone and hope to better the 100 metre sprint world record. In order to achieve that, Faith needs to be backed by ideas that provide a clear path towards that goal. So, if the goal is to become a sprint champion, then the thoughts should contain ideas about fitness, workouts, schedules, diets and then self visualizations that consist of the performances that are closer to the reality that we want to achieve.

The mind is bombarded with signals all the time, rushing in and diving like a raging waterfall, flooding the it completely, manifesting in many different ways, and pulling us in several directions, some so mutually contradictory that we're not sure of what we are really doing or the purpose of our actions. It is possible to be stunned into inaction, blank and unproductive, and unable to get a handle on what is supposed to be accomplished. But what is really impacting the mind, and our actions, is the inability to understand the thoughts that are driving our actions in the moment, and the influences that are leading to the thoughts originating in the mind. We also tend to see life through our own unique lenses. This is something that we call the '**mindset**' – the unique set of assumptions and expectations which we hold about ourselves, our lives and the situations around us. In reality, these mindsets that we hold on to, will play a significant role in determining our thoughts, actions, and hence some of our life's outcomes, and also how we perceive and engage with others and the universe around us. Reflecting within ourselves to understand, adapt and modify or change the mindset, can help us to drastically change a lot of aspects of our lives, such as improve the health, decrease the stress levels and evolve into something more resilient to life's challenges.

It is not possible to control the external world around us, and align it with our own goals and objectives. And though it seems easy, it is not also simple and straightforward that we are automatically in full control of everything that goes on within us. All the thoughts that arise within us are the product of influences driven by the world external to us, as well as our **innate beliefs**, **prejudices**, and our **unique genetics**. But deep engagement with our minds can help us to understand what is filling up the mind, and how these are aligned to our goals and objectives in life.

Our innate mindsets can be helpful for distilling information, managing expectations, and guard us from slipping into undesirable states of mind. But the mindsets that we hold can also be maladaptive, lead to interpersonal problems and feelings of guilt, inadequacy, sadness and anxiety. We have to appreciate that in the dynamic course of life, that could take several shapes and forms rapidly, there is no constant with regard to the mindset or the mind. A set of thoughts that might have been very helpful to drive our actions in a certain point in time, may not be the most appropriate for another stage in life. If we take the example of our youth, there are several actions which we pursue with glee, carrying a particular mindset, but which could be entirely out of place in a different phase of life.

"Just as the lotus rises to the level of water, so too does a man's

stature rises up to the level of his thoughts"

– The Thirukkural

And so, the power to determine what we become, and how we get there, is solely vested with us. The path to building a concrete sense of purpose and aligning our actions to achieve the sense of purpose, is built on the bedrock of the thoughts that fill the mind. Or, rather it is the thoughts which we fill our minds with. It is so because, our mindsets are highly conducive to changes if we keep closely engaging with the thoughts, watch for thoughts that prevent us from evolving and defeat those distorted thoughts.

We can equate the mind to the courtyard or an open patch on the ground. This space has potential to turn into several different possibilities. If left uncared, and to itself, the space could sprout wild grasses, and weeds, filling itself up with anything that is thrust on it by the forces of nature. However, under careful curated landscaping or gardening, the small patch could turn into a space of beauty or a garden full of fruits and vegetables. The difference is that the space is filled with care, and looked after to ensure that it stays that way, for it is still not immune to being acted upon by other forces. So, it is not sufficient to plant or sow the patch with chosen vegetation, but care should also be taken to ensure that anything that does not belong to that patch, does not find its way into the patch and sprout.

Such is the nature of the mind as well – that you can identify the thoughts that are aligned to the core purpose, and nurture such thoughts, while also filtering the ones that get into the mind and demand attention. There should be an acute cognizance of what are the thoughts that manifest, because, not being in control leads to manifestations that are not aligned to the core purpose, and disrupts the progress towards a goal or leads to the path itself going astray.

The placebo and nocebo effects, used in pharmaceutical clinical research, are very good illustrations of what could happen when the mind tends to dwell on the external influences that could shape thoughts. These effects have a large root in a person's expectations. If we are sufficiently impressed to expect certain outcomes, by people in who we have faith, then such inputs can go a long way towards influencing our perceptions towards the outcomes. Therefore, if we expect a pill to make us feel better, based on the advise of doctors in who we trust, we may feel better after taking it. And equally, in case of the contrary, which is referred to as the Nocebo effect.

The mind and the thoughts contained in it are well within our control to shape and filter, if we are able to elevate our self awareness, understand what is manifesting as our personality and drawing other influences towards us. A soldier seeks to elevate the thoughts that manifest as valour, commitment, loyalty and alertness, while an athlete seeks to elevate the thoughts that manifest as passion, discipline, optimism and perfectionism. It will not behove a soldier to elevate a passion to wage war, though it perfectly behoves an athlete to elevate the passion to compete backed by perfectionism in execution . So also, an athlete will not help her cause by elevating valour in place of discipline and optimism.

It is entirely in our control to chose the thoughts that define our purpose, the objectives underpinning the purpose and the path to propel us towards achieving the goals and objectives. And once we have this clarity, we have to engage the mind to ensure that these thoughts are continuously shaped by the right set of internal and external influences. It is this that makes the difference between whether the mind turns out to be the well landscaped patch cultivated to look and feel in a particular manner, or a wild patch that bends and stretches to the demands of numerous influences finding its way towards it.

Lack of Success is not due to Lack of Skill or Money, it is due to Lack of Karma !

Sometimes in life, there may be problems and failures due to lack of positive karma but for a positive reason, because they are the biggest blessings provided by the divine power to make you & the world around you realize that you are more bigger than what you think!

– His Holiness Shri Aasaanji

DREAMS & IMAGINATION – THE POWER OF VISUALIZATION

Stay Focused, Dream Big !

One of the highest powers of the human being is the power to dream!

Dream is the invisible power which keeps us away from the bad past..

And creates a great future!

Those who consciously create a big dream will create a great future.....

Not only for themselves, But also for the entire humanity!

Let the world keep screaming, you keep dreaming, now success will be streaming every time and in every aspect of life

Energy draining vocal expression has got no power when compared to energy gaining visual impression that is happening in meditation

– His Holiness Shri Aasaanji

"It's a dream come true!" is an oft repeated statement, heard in the context of several different situations ranging from getting to see something / someone, to doing something successfully, to achieving a particular goal. It is a statement that is usually made as a vindication of a firmly held belief or an expression of unflinching faith. However, no matter what drives the statement, an inescapable conclusion is that the event or outcome has been fondly held in the mind, with a lot of importance attached, carefully nurtured, and constantly reinforced through positive associations.

"Chance favours the prepared mind"

– Louis Pasteur

If Louis Pasteur doesn't know this, then no one else in the world will, because he is the one who single handedly changed the definition of how we look at microbes and their impact on causing diseases in humans. And in the process, he invented the life-saving vaccination technique which we all take for granted as something that is very commonplace to our lives. However, try to imagine what it would have been during the days when humanity was oblivious to such a possibility that could save lives. Would it have originated, had Pasteur not imagined and visualized a concept hitherto not known to any human. It is a thought that originated inside him, and he kept this thought close and precious, meditated on it to such an extent that he was ready to capture the outcome the moment it materialized.

Pasteur's was a prepared mind that had visualized something which had no precedent in human history, the shape, form or appearance of which was not known hitherto. But his mind held the right set of thoughts that informed him of this possibilities, because of which he knew what to expect and anticipate.

This is but just one instance in the great annals of scientific progress. From Copernicus to Archimedes to Newton to Pasteur to Edison to Einstein, the world will not be what it is today but for the **power of visualization** which were fed by the dreams and imaginations of great individuals. None of these greats were focused on an outcome but were powered by the visualization of their dreams and imaginations, powerful thoughts that have advanced humanity.

We should not, however, mistake this to mean that we should be led by the outcomes alone, because that would lead to the mind losing track of the 'here & now', and foregrounding the future, leading to misplaced priorities in the mind.

But, what this does entail is, holding a view of the desired outcome puts us that much closer to our goals and objectives, that it reduces the distance to the achievement, makes it seem very reachable and strengthen the sense of purpose. It will help to ensure that the thoughts aligned to the outcome are all synchronized. Further, by making the fruits of labour more palpable, visualization attaches a positive connotation to the thoughts and gives an impetus to the progress towards one's goals.

It is the path to being the person or personality that you want to be – ie the ability visualize yourself in such a position, either executing the task or enjoying the outcomes. It is an attestation of the immense power of the mind, that visualization helps us to gravitate towards the right manifestations and thoughts that drive such manifestations, as also get closer to the people and things that will be an inherent part of what we want to achieve.

As much as focusing on the right thoughts in our mind takes us closer to what we want, visualizing the actions and the process will also help to identify the deficiencies in the path to achievement, and act as a enlightened self-critic, helping to refine the course of action, and identify newer thoughts to fill the mind with.

"More than taking pride in wielding an arrow that killed a rabbit, is holding a spear that was aimed at an elephant which escaped yet"

– The Thirukkural

A mind, that is focusing on a certain set of thoughts centred around getting to a specific goal, is relentlessly exploring every minute task and such details associated with getting to the goal. In addition to getting much closer to the goal, the mind is also setting itself up by way of practice, rehearsals and familiarization. An enhanced level of focus on thoughts aligned to something specific means that the actual execution of the task occurs with pre-programmed precision because such is the power of the mind that it has gone through each step, aligned the right set of thoughts, in the right order, and envisaged the possibilities.

This is why sportspersons and performers leverage visualization as a core aspect of their training and preparations. How much ever prepared the athlete is, the reality of being in front a crowd of thousands, and surrounded by all the competitors, is not a very easy state to be in. No matter how much one wants to stay positive, and block out all the thoughts about things that could go wrong, the mind could still be filled with self-doubt, and questions. Visualization is a powerful tool that can enable such a performer to create a strong mental image of the situation, filling it with thoughts of success, over powering the thoughts associated with failures and challenges.

Dreams and imaginations are powerful devices to bring the thoughts together in the mind, and produce the right outcomes when leveraged in the right fashion. However much care should be taken to ensure that such visualizations are focused on the fruits of success, rather than the pains of failures. Such is the power of the mind that a negative connotation attached to a thought could act as a weight dragging us backwards instead of nudging or propelling us forward.

"Don't disturb me, I'm playing chess." - Natan Sharansky's jailers took that as powerful evidence that he was going - or had already become - quite mad. Natan Sharansky was a former Soviet dissident who was jailed on charges of treason and sentenced to solitary confinement in a Siberian jail, which extended for a period of 9 years. He was locked up in a punishment cell that had no bed, chair or table, leave alone a chessboard and pieces. He emerged from the confinement, not only entirely sane, but also went on to beat the world chess champion Gary Kasaparov in

an exhibition game, and also ended up as a minister in the Government of Israel, winning popular elections. Sharansky visualized himself playing thousands of chess games, switching sides and constantly executing these moves in the mind, keeping the mind engaged, sane and active, contrary to the expectations of his captors.

The biggest strength of all, when it comes to the state of mind, is the power of self-belief. Dreams and visualizations serve to strengthen self-belief, reinforcing the idea that an achievement is not beyond our abilities and enabling us to constantly remind ourselves that we are on the right track and progressing. It is because the process brings more clarity on what we want, why we want it and how we will go about getting it.

As our senses get bombarded by several signals, which cause a torrential flow of thoughts in the mind, the most important thing to do is to ensure that the pre-determined, natural flow of thoughts do not get altered, just as a river could flood its banks and change course when subjected to a deluge. Visualizing keeps us on the right path, not only by giving is the clarity in action, but also by serving as a lighthouse in the storm, preventing us from veering of course and into the rocks.

The mind makes it possible to explore the limits of our capabilities, as long as we harness its immense potential to not only align the right set of thoughts to guide our actions, but also use the power of dreams and imagination to visualize ourselves in the right state of manifestations. No goal is beyond reach and an insurmountable challenge as long as we see ourselves in such states that are desirable to get to these goals. We are only what we imagine ourselves to be and are only limited by our power to imagine.

The highest need for success is not skill or money,
its your ability to focus on your Vision!
The ultimate & fundamental difference between
humans and animals, is living with a sense of
purpose...
And, a desire about the future!

– His Holiness Shri Aasaanji

An Exponent of Vedic Science, Upanishad and Holy Scriptures, Guruji's life-changing teachings & techniques are non-religious and imbibe contemporary scientific principles. They are designed to instantly liberate a person from the impact of misconceived beliefs, negativity, and conditioned habits which limit the potential to enjoy life to the fullest.

His Holiness Shri Aasaanji has rediscovered the timeless wisdom of ancient spiritual texts, to enhance inner wellbeing, and experience unstoppable success and happiness, touching all aspects of human life and making it easier to achieve everlasting peace, health, wealth and prosperity.

DISCIPLINE – THE ART OF CHANNELIZING YOUR THOUGHTS TOWARDS HAPPINESS

PUSH YOURSELF...
Because no one else is going to do that for you!!

Push yourselves to reach greater heights....

You will never know your real power,

Unless you push yourself to a bigger dream.

Everything you wanted is already within you...

The life you want to live is waiting for your decision

that comes with 100% commitment & determination!

– His Holiness Shri Aasaanji

Habits – a word that could take one right back to childhood and trigger a flood of memories, which are sometimes sweet and sometimes not so! We go through a lot of actions in our every day lives, without realizing or consciously engaging the mind and thought to execute such actions. These are what we characterize as habits. And the power of habits is that we go through those actions without having to think about the how or what or the why – we never take time to think about whether or not to brush our teeth as soon as we wake up from the night's sleep; if not the first action, at least there will be no question about whether we need to brush or not!

A good part of our daily lives are driven by our habits; right from basics like personal hygiene and grooming on one hand, to eating, exercising, and to even meditating for some people. If we really retrospect, we will realize that none of these habits came to manifest without any effort. The habits that people carry were taught either formally or informally, or picked up through conscious and / or unconscious observations. However, if we step back a bit and look into ourselves, we will realize that we did not pick up 'habits', but what we have really picked up are behaviours that seemed stylish or appealing and which we wanted to imitate to appear as endearing as the one from whom we learned. Most of these may be from people around us, and some mannerisms from on-screen characters who we admired. But it takes 'disciplined repetition' to ensure that a behaviour moves up along the chain to become a practice or a routine and turn into a habit.

Repetition lies at the root of **habit formation**, even for the most simplest of actions like personal hygiene. And a firm resolve or motivation, backed by a commitment to the self is the key to repetition. Repetition driven by commitment is brought about only by self-discipline. Even something as simple as brushing the teeth the first thing in the morning, did not come about without any of these being in place – resolve or commitment and discipline. Most behaviours turn into habits in response to fear of negative consequences, like brushing, while some are inspired by our own will to make a change in ourselves.

Resolve or motivation is the manifestation of an unwavering focus on what we want to achieve; our goals and objectives, and our unique dreams and imaginations. Though we do not realize it, maintaining our own personal hygiene is a result of the same unwavering focus on not being perceived as repulsive. Our actions oriented towards achieving this state of being non-repulsive, is not a very consciously executed set of actions, but a set of simple habits, the motivations, actions, consequences of which that are so deeply ingrained into the mind that they are executed without any conscious engagement with the mind. It is the power of the mind that enables us to exist and manifest in this manner – enabling actions that seem very benign and effortless.

Now, imagine a very well trained and an expert hunter, very well versed in the ways of the forest and possessing good deal of skill in wielding the equipment required on the job. And let's consider that the hunter has been deputed to recover / retrieve an animal that has gone rogue and is disrupting routine lives around the forest – we've heard a lot of such stories about tigers, leopards, elephants that were tranquilized, captured and safely let out in areas that are safe for the animals, as well as human inhabitations around them. A hunter, in such a scenario, moves through the forest terrain, looking for tell – tale signs of the animals' presence, identifies its tracks, seeks out potential hide – outs, and will know where and how to set trap and wait. As a complete outsider to this situation, and not being a possessor of all such skills, a confident lay person will probably be able to do the same actions, but equipped with a very comprehensive guide and constantly referring back and forth to ensure that no step is missed or a precaution not taken. However, if we are able to watch a hunter at work, we may probably observe that all these actions happen without the slightest hint of effort, as if it were like waking up in the morning and brushing the teeth.

It is not just a hunter; perhaps an experienced marathon runner who knows where to accelerate and where to hold steady, or a swimmer or a pilot or an expert driver, and so forth. Any of these people could be found indulging in actions that are not driven by conscious thought or consideration, but as if propelled by some unseen force guiding their movements and causing the actions, better known as a force of habit.

We may resolve to achieve something or be highly motivated to get to a desired state, whether it is the state of hygiene or health or education or career. However, what really sets apart the achievers from the also-ran, is the pursuit of means to get to the goal. We may want to get to a particular position, but will not get there unless we're well aware of the means to get there. Our commitment to the goal or achievement is underpinned by the ability to identify the resources and knowledge, and the various steps in the process of getting there. Empowering ourselves with such resources amounts to committing ourselves to act on the resolve. Thus, the knowledge, and the process to leverage the knowledge, become two key pillars that are holding up our commitment and resolve.

Discipline is the third pillar that completes this foundation, and the most significant one. Discipline is nothing but executing a set of routines or patterns diligently, and with conviction. The routines will weave together the desired behaviours, knowledge and resources, behind the resolve, and add the context of self-awareness to prevent road-blocks and ensure progress.

"The whole point is to discipline the mind"

– Swami Vivekananda

It is critical to note that discipline is not just a product of focusing on the right behaviours alone. We will not be able to manifest the right behaviours if we do not take into account the innate strengths and weaknesses. We have to align our strengths to drive us in the right directions, but most importantly have to ensure that the discipline addresses any weaknesses that could hinder or obstruct progress.

The mind of so powerful that nothing is beyond reach, but it is only as powerful as we will let it be. If we chose to not accept a weakness, then we will end up failing to build the right discipline and, in turn, it will prevent us from forming the habits that will take us towards our goals.

Success is not the outcome of hard work or knowledge or access to resources. Success is the outcome of forming the right set of habits backed by persistence, consistency and driven by knowledge and other resources. Success is achieved by focusing the mind on diligent self-discipline in pursuing and executing the actions that are imperative for the desired outcomes. Success is also in not getting carried away by impulses, and exercising self-control (another way to look at discipline) that we do not get distracted from the immediate tasks at hand and are able to complete those satisfactorily, satisfaction leading to happiness, as is implicitly known, felt and appreciated.

The benefit of forming habits is that we give our minds more space to think about the exceptions that occur in the path towards the desired outcomes. Discipline that leads to formation of habits, reduces the number of decisions that have to be made, thereby freeing up the mind to address the unexpected. The key benefit, is that the mind will gradually become less noisy, allowing for improved focus and clarity, leaving more space to focus on the important thoughts and process them in a calm and unhurried manner, giving ourselves the right space and time to accomplish and complete.

Our daily lives are filled with decisions of many kinds – some small with immediate impact, and some that are humongous with a life-long impact. Each and every day of our lives is a course that drives us through several such moments that involve these decisions. And each decision involves processing several thoughts in the minds, weighing the implications, the nature of outcomes and their criticality to our lives. This course through decisions starts from the moment that we are awake, involving, for some, questions around breakfast and attire while for some others, it may revolve around whom to meet for completing certain tasks.

We learn a lot of things through the course of lives, as children, as young adults, and as adults with broader responsibilities in the society – namely being parents, workers, professionals, managers, and individuals who are part of a community. We're taught, as children, to inculcate habits and manners that concern hygiene and morals. As young adults, we are taught, and learn the value of education, good health, and civility. And as adults we learn and imbibe the responsibilities of being part of families, professions, organizations, and the citizenry, managing and participating in activities underpinning each of these, addressing our own well-being and that of the people around us, as well as the society. Decisions are an inherent part of all these phases, some routine and simple and some exceptional and complex.

Every decision will involve executing tasks and actions, which draw on our knowledge, experience, as well as fears and anxieties about possible outcomes. Our happiness hinges on the ability to simplify this process by reducing the number of decisions which we have to make, by adopting the right set of behaviours, building routines around these behaviours, practicing disciplined adoption of these routines and converting them into habits. Habits are very much akin to our muscles. The muscles that we build enable us to be more active, thus strengthening themselves in the process as well as allowing other muscles to evolve. Similarly, habits are the muscles driving us on the path to happiness through discipline and control. Habits, discipline and self – control are not just aspects that ease our path to achieving our goals. But they also play a key role in ensuring happiness along this path. Practicing these consistently will lead to more clarity on what to do and what not, which, enable us to avoid conflicts that could lead to negative emotions. Further, in addition to giving us more space and clarity, discipline also ensures that the short – term actions do not impact any longer term goals, ensuring happiness and satisfaction which is more permanent and sustainable.

We have seen that, a critical part of achieving our goals is to achieve clarity in the mind about the right set of thoughts to be aligned. However, it is imperative that we back these with conviction and drive a disciplined way of engaging these thoughts, manifesting the right set of behaviours, without having to bog ourselves down at each step by the necessity to make decisions. Reducing the stress of having to make decisions at every step will automatically relieve the mind and create the space for peace and quiet, and hence, everlasting happiness.

Rise Yourself To Rise Others!

The only way to create peace is to find
peace within your own self
Its time to grow... time to change
"RISE YOURSELF.....TO RISE OTHERS"

– His Holiness Shri Aasaanji

www.atmayoga.in

HARNESSING THE POWER OF INNER SELF – DRIVING POSITIVITY

Self-Enquiry (Atma Vicharam)- The One Only Gateway to Eternal Peace & Success !

Self-enquiry is not talking to others or talking about others...

It is talking to your own self and listening to your own self;

This will give you the power to bring unstoppable positive changes...

In the present and to the future!

And will protect you in the present from the bad impacts of past sin

and keep you away from future sins

– His Holiness Shri Aasaanji

Inner power is the quiet force within you that knows when to act and when to move and gives you the strength to do so. This inner power is something we all have, but we need to learn how to tap into it in creative and effective ways in our daily life. Tapping into our inner power to stay true to our real self is at the root of reducing inner conflicts and tapping the power to achieve. Every one of us is one of a kind. A tiger never asks itself, "Why am I not as big as an elephant?" Each part of creation has its own beauty and its own strengths.

The inner self is about what can't be seen: feelings, intuition, values, beliefs, personality, thoughts, emotions, fantasies, spirituality, desire, and purpose. A strong inner self means that we cope well with our emotions, are self-aware, have clarity and a good sense of our values, and feel a purpose in life. It also means that we are able to remain calm and resilient in the face of adversity from the outer world.

How much of the time are we "running on empty," just struggling to get through the demands of the day, without considering whether our actions and behaviours are in line with our inner self? The conflict between the two selves can result in stress, which makes us more vulnerable to illness – both physical as well as mental. Our daily functioning may also be affected. We may feel successful on the outside but empty on the inside. When this happens, we are also be at risk for quick fixes to heal our pain, such as turning to drugs or alcohol or other distractions that take attention away from the core challenge, but give an artificial feeling of elation.

The tension between the inner self and outer self is common in the modern world. Each of us is tugged in multiple directions every day and our actions and behaviours do not always align with our core values as a result. However, becoming aware of our inner-self and how it balances with our outer self is the foundation for good mental, physical, and spiritual health. This is why it is an important aspect to consider when working on a good balance in our life.

We saw that decisions are a very critical and inherent part of our daily lives – from simple ones to very complex ones. And we understood the fact that reducing the number of decisions we make is a means of achieving a more peaceful existence, and hence happiness. Engaging the inner self is a critical aspect in reducing conflict, avoiding needless decisions and harnessing our abilities better.

A career choice is a very simple example of how the conflict with the inner self plays out. We're presented with a job opportunity, with all its usual trappings; ie company profile, salary package, role, power & authority, etc. Typically, in such situations, in most of the cases, the decision will hinge on a lot of external influences such as the brand name of the company, the job location, the material benefits that the job will bring along the way, and external perceptions associated with the role. It is very rare that this evaluation is made in the context of the inner self which constitutes the innate values, strengths, principles, beliefs, and such aspects which make the person unique.

This is not an unique happening and is very common to most people, in most situations – that we end up being a product of the environment and the external influences, rather than being a product of who we really are. We experience a lot of conflicts because we try to be what we are expected to be, rather than accept who we really are and shape ourselves in accordance with this inner self. We are all tuned to describe ourselves using the labels given to us by our external environment – our qualifications, our professions, our roles in the society, our belongings, and we tend to believe in this deeply and identify ourselves accordingly.

Many of us have an inner dialogue that says, "I'm not good enough" or "I don't deserve it" or

"I don't have it in me." This usually comes from years of listening to other people's opinions of us—overcritical parents, jealous coworkers, competitive siblings, and others.

"You are the visible & invisible
You are the seen & unseen
and you are the manifested & unmanifested
You are not a drop contained in the ocean,
you are the drop that
contain the entire ocean in a drop."

– Chandogya Upanishad

The ocean is not a unitary, homogenous entity. It is a multi-dimensional, heterogenous entity, but consisting of several strata that are unitary, homogenous entities themselves, very different from each other. Each strata of the ocean is a complete ecosystem in itself.

The mind is, in many ways, similar, and as deep and rich as the ocean, with its depths and expanse. Our ability to tap into its depths determines the extent to which we are able to pursue goals and objectives. This means silent contemplation and allowing the thoughts to bubble to the top, identifying the right set of thoughts to engage with, separating the external influences from the internal forces that actually stand for who we are. The ocean reveals its depths only when the waves slow down and there is less disturbance on the surface. Similarly, for the inner self to reveal itself, the mind's thoughts have to slow down in their frequency and intensity.

Meditation offers an opportunity to change your life, from the source – the thoughts – and manifest the dreams. Meditation provides an opportunity to engage the inner self better and build the right bridge with the outer world. Meditation is the path towards better mindfulness, enabling a transformation from tactical survival to a deeper and a wider engagement with the universe, on one's own terms, leading to an existence that is devoid of knee-jerk and emotional reactions, to one with a more conscious interaction. Meditation enables harnessing the inner-self to power the path towards achieving the goals, by enabling an acceptance of the past and envisioning a desired future, holding together positive and self-reinforcing thoughts in the mind.

Always Remember Stillness in Meditation is the Ultimate Oneness with the Divine!

The ultimate truth of Atmayoga is not just
the stillness of

meditation, but One-ness with the divine where
inner-self is not

different from the supreme self;

The ultimate state of human consciousness

Always remember stillness in meditation is
the ultimate oneness with the divine

– His Holiness Shri Aasaanji

www.atmayoga.in

TIME, EXPECTATIONS AND IMAGINATION – DRIVERS OF THOUGHTS AND BEHAVIOURS

> The thought, the ability to think, is a gift
> to humans...
>
> Your observation of a thought will make
> you aware that
>
> it is shaped either by time or a predetermined
> expectation...
>
> And the expectations are in turn consequences
> of your past experience, imaginations, and desires...
>
> Understanding this will help you to shape
> or reshape the
>
> thought to derive meaning in life!
>
> **– His Holiness Shri Aasaanji**

From time immemorial, to where we are now, humanity has been constantly driven by the search for 'truth'; truth not being a singular, unitary definition but a highly contextual one, or a philosophy. In every walk of life, 'truth' is a set of ideas or beliefs that seem to best explain the phenomena of that area. We are all subject to those. Science considers something confirmed by proof to be the truth. However, such truth is only objective in the context of our perceptions and perspectives. Newton's theory of gravity was assumed to be universally applicable, till Einstein's theory of relativity, which provided a more definitive context for how and where gravity works.

As society evolves and new ideas emerge, giving rise to the need to define truth, or interpret it with regard to context. It is explained by our tendency to seek several opinions on several areas of our daily lives. We all never hesitate to go to one or more experts for second opinions on a vast variety of issues concerning our daily lives, from health to finance to property to education and even leisure holidays! It is in our nature to not go with the spontaneous and guard ourselves from the known and the unknown unknowns!

"Every trouble is temporary and peace is permanent; peace is possible only when you know the truth, the truth is there Is god and the God is Within You!"

– His Holiness Shri Aasaanji

Many a time we seek opinions to validate our own innate thoughts and preferences, but we also seek opinions to be sure that we have not missed something that may have been very obvious. But how is it that we miss the obvious, and we do miss such things on more than few occasions.

Is It a special skill that allows someone to see what another expert missed, like an extra sensory perception ? Not really an extra sensory power, but certainly an ability to perceive beyond the usual. How could a person be bestowed with such a skill or ability ? It is simply a case of having seen, experienced and learned more, that there is the ability to **imagine** and **expect** something that others may have missed.

Imagination is the most powerful feature of humanity, which has seen us transcend the state of our origins, survive the wild, and build massive civilizations. It is no coincidence that all these civilizations of the past, though they thrived in isolation with very little contact and sharing of knowledge, still have very similar elements, be it religious beliefs or infrastructure development or scientific discoveries. It was possible only because of the inherent commonality among us humans – the power to imagine.

Whist imagination gives us the ability to perceive the unseen and unknown, we are also bestowed with the great ability to perceive through our past experiences. This ability, though much more common than those powered by imagination, is a bigger driver of our everyday manifestations, and actions thereof. It is also what made some of the humans to elevate themselves beyond the rest and achieve greatness or uniqueness. All this is driven by a very mundane but powerful feature that we're endowed with, right from the moment we are born into this world – the power to expect.

A great deal of the thoughts that arise and manifest as actions, are a product of our ability to perceive the world, driven by the power to imagine and the power to expect. At the outset, this may seem very insignificant and commonplace in the larger context of events that make up our lives. However, a deeper introspection will enable us to understand how our thoughts and hence our behaviours have been a product of our imaginations and our expectations.

It will be very Illustrative to think of a typical day, and how the expectations based on past experiences, and imaginations based on our learnings, are often the major drivers of how the day started, progressed and ended. Some of us may have the habit of waking up to the morning cuppa (coffee or milk or a herbal drink, as the case may be). A few of us may be lucky enough to have someone prepare this for us, and there may be others who prefer to prepare this for themselves. There is a possibility of waking up to find this missing or not being in a position to prepare it due to any of the several reasons like ingredient not being available, or so forth. It is quite common for many people to get frustrated at this occurrence, though we may well be aware that it will not make the slightest difference to our physical or mental existence in any way. But yet we may let ourselves be overwhelmed by this negative thought, manifesting as a negative emotion, influencing further behaviours and actions, and potentially leaving us with a very bad day.

It Is quite common for many people to wake up to their social media, official messages and the news of the day. And even before we realize it, we're bombarded with a burst of inputs and sensations that target all parts of the brain. It may be something as simple as a traffic update that leads us to imagine the route which has to be taken to avoid potential chaos, to a good or a bad occurrence at work that could trigger an imagination about the nature of workplace on that day, or a very random typical, and showy message from someone in the contact list that could trigger a feeling of personal success or inadequacy, leading one to imagine their situation positively or negatively. While seeming very innocuous, a simple introspection will show us how we may have let our imaginations run wild at the start of a day, which in turn led to several thoughts manifesting in behaviours and actions, some progressive and productive, while most could have been regressive and carrying a negative impact on the state of the mind, the thoughts that come out of it and the actions they influence.

Now, expectations and imaginations are not the only factors that drive and determine our thinking, behaviours and actions thereof. There is one more very unique factor that drives our thinking. Our ability to track and manage **time !** A very simple illustration is the food habits that have been cultivated in us over time. It is very common behaviour to see people head for food based on the time of the day, and not based on whether the body demands food or not. Animals seek food when they are hungry, but humans are conditioned to seek food based on the time of the day. And then there are several other events in a day that are triggered by time, like going to school or work, or many other daily tasks like exercise or prayer and so on.

It Is vital to understand the role played by these three major factors - time, expectation, and imagination – in triggering our thoughts and the way they manifest in our daily lives. In a way, we often end up being prisoners of our expectations derived from past experiences, the imaginations triggered by our insights and knowledge, and pre-determined habits.

Neuro science indicates that the human brain has an overwhelming tendency to generate habitual behaviour, by unleashing systems that can takeover massive amount of neural resources and driving us to function programmatically, causing us to function and behave in the same ways as we've done before. However, the good news is that this tendency of the brain is not cast in stone and it has the potential to rewire itself, albeit through conscious effort. It is this flexibility that allows us to retain control over our thoughts, and actions, though this ability (flexibility) declines as we grow through childhood, into adolescence and later. The ability to be flexible, and rewire itself, is not seen anywhere bigger than in the case of the coronavirus pandemic of 2020-2022, when humanity as a whole adjusted itself into a completely different way of existence, assisted by technology in even the most intrinsic behaviours like communicating.

"My expectations were reduced to zero when I was 21. Everything since then has been a bonus."

– Stephen Hawking

No one else can exemplify the nature of existing without expectations, and in defying habituation, than Stephen Hawking, the most celebrated scientist who lived across the 20th and 21st centuries. As "Nature", the renowned science magazine puts it:

"When Stephen Hawking was diagnosed with motor-neuron disease at the age of 21, it wasn't clear that he would finish his PhD. Against all expectations, he lived on for 55 years, becoming one of the world's most celebrated scientists.

In 1985, Stephen Hawkings underwent a tracheotomy, which removed his already limited powers of speech. He was able to control a cursor on a screen and type out sentences — albeit with increasingly painful slowness (first with his hand, and eventually only with a cheek muscle). A speech synthesizer processed his words and generated the androidal accent that became his trademark. In this way, he completed his best-selling book A Brief History of Time.

Stephen remained remarkably positive throughout his life, despite the immense frustration that his condition clearly caused. He enjoyed theatre and opera trips, and he seemed energized rather than exhausted by his travels to all parts of the world, as well as by his regular trips to the California Institute of Technology in Pasadena. He retained robust common sense and a sense of humour, expressed forceful opinions, supported political causes and was happy to engage with the media."

Indeed, as Stephen Hawking puts it, his ability to reduce expectations to zero has been a significant bonus both to himself and to the rest of humanity who were enlightened by the significant progress that he made in the realm of physics. It boggles the mind to imagine the state of progress in our understanding of this universe, if Stephen Hawkings had instead sought to bury himself under the weight of the expectations that he thought he couldn't have met, due to the disease that afflicted him.

Having been given just a few years to live, that may have dealt a blow to his own expectations, and faced with a life that was beyond his control, the flexibility displayed should be considered phenomenal, not only it came from a zest to exist, but it was not a mere existence, but a life of immense meaning both to the self as well as to all of humanity. It is plainly evident that the flexibility not only removed a set of barriers to existence, which could otherwise have caused distress and frustration, but the flexibility actually provided the ability to continue engaging with the world on his own terms, thus enabling him to derive satisfaction from scientific progress and build an inner strength to persevere.

So, is the case for each of us. If we're able to display flexibility in the face of our brain's tendency to push us towards habituated behaviours, or desist from getting carried away by expectations that are a result of past experiences, and understand that imagination is a guide for our actions and not the outcomes that define our actions, it is very easy to take life as it happens and react to it in the most appropriate manner and not in a preset fashion.

What happens, happens to everybody,
but what happens to you is decided only by you...

It is never too late for anybody to have
a new thought; to dream

a new dream; make a new belief and
live a great life!!

– His Holiness Shri Aasaanji

The most common experience one hears from Guruji's followers is their ability to manifest and co-create their lives by their own design. They live their lives at cause rather than at the effect of circumstances and are victorious rather than victims of their circumstances.

ABOUT THE AUTHOR

His Holiness Shri Aasaanji is a World-Renowned, Non-Religious, Contemporary Spiritual Leader, Global Humanitarian, A Great Visionary and Living Enlightened Master of Inner-Science & Ancient wisdom.

Empowering Humanity

Founder of the Atmayoga Foundation-One Human Family (an Institute for Inner-Science and Self-Transformation), Guruji is globally known as a practical spiritualist hailing from India, spreading Global Peace through Inner-Peace.

Shri Aasaanji's life changing teachings and techniques are non-religious, totally scientific and contemporary, For more than 2 Decades, Millions of people across the globe have Experienced Miracles through his Divine Presence & Powerful Spiritual Teachings.

Shri Aasaanji's students & Followers are spread across the globe India, USA, UK, Malaysia, Sri Lanka, Singapore, Canada, Australia and the Middle East, that includes people from all walks of life including Medical Doctors, Spiritual Masters, Entrepreneurs, Educationists, Entertainers, Global Leaders, Policy makers and various public personalities who hail him for his guidance and teachings for total well-being & Holistic success.

A living embodiment of spiritual knowledge and healing power, Guruji makes us realise that every human being is a gift of God with incredible self-healing power, and, is a positive change agent to create a better future with peace, brother hood and harmony. He makes us aware that in God's creation there is no discrimination and always draws attention to the fact that the Supreme Power is one and same for everyone and that we all belong to One Human Family.

Guruji always insists that knowledge is nothing without action; and constantly reinforces the fact that practice makes you progress. His approach is to instil the belief that every human being is blessed by nature with the power to see the invisible, to do the Impossible, and to achieve the unbelievable - Believe in Miracles; Commitment is the Secret is the core tenet of his message !!

His Holiness Shri Aasaanji has rediscovered the timeless wisdom of ancient spiritual science to experience unstoppable success & happiness in all aspects of human life with everlasting peace, health, wealth & prosperity easier than ever before.

Guruji is an Exponent of the Shiva Sutras, Vedic Science, Upanishad, Brahma Sutra, Naturopathy and Inner Well-being.

Master Of Inner-Science & Ancient Wisdom for Self-Transformation

His Holiness Shri Aasaanji is the creator of transformational practices such as Prana-Vritti & Atma-dhyana designed to empower humanity with great health and the ability to be the architect of one's own destiny.

Guruji explains the timeless energy technique & self-Transformation method with the most simple & Uncomplicated clarity through his spiritual wisdom which he has attained by self-realisation of the ultimate Inner-Power & Cosmic Vibration.

His Holiness Shri Aasaanji has transformed the lives of his innumerable followers. Being most scientific and practical, his teachings can be practiced irrespective of a person's religion, race, gender, caste or community. Guruji's disciples say his very presence brings a transformational positive shift in their lives.

Following his teaching they experience improved health, closer & more meaningful relationships, greater self-confidence, wealth and energy levels.

Atma-Dhyana

Atma-Dhyana is the most powerful process to experience inner-transformation and to rewrite your destiny. It leads the path to overcome negativity and negative karma and be the architect of one's own destiny and achieve the life one wants to live.

Created and initiated by Shri Aasaanji, Atma-Dhyana is the extra-ordinary science of Inner-transformation to unleash a human's ultimate power and create abundance and fulfilment in all aspects of life. It is a life-transforming meditation & mind-tuning psychic practice to attain conscious connection with the inner-self and experience the Divine within.

Atma-Dhyana helps free one from fears and pain of the past, helps eliminate negative energies and negative karma from current and past lives and gives one the power to create a future of peace, success and happiness.

"Your Life is Pre-Written, but with Clear Vision and Meditation it can be Re-Written"

Countless people have been able to regain their lost health, wealth and happiness in relationships after following this path-breaking practice.

Prana-Vritti

Prana-Vritti is the most effective wellness workshop that has transformed lives of innumerable people by helping them easily regain their lost health & happiness without the aid of medicines. Prana-Vritti is practiced and recommended by eminent medical doctors and wellness therapist in India and the world over. Prana-Vritti is a powerful energy technique designed to trigger in built instructions to activate the body's own inner intelligence & natural healing power. The practice assures the prevention & cure from several incurable & irreversible health conditions. It increases the flow of life energy in all energy centers (chakra) & energy channel (Nadis) which unfailingly improves the functions of corresponding Internal organs, Nervous & Endocrine system which is essential for everlasting vibrant health. Prana-vritti is a penultimate solution for all lifestyle diseases (Blood pressure, Cholesterol, Diabetes, Heart disorder etc) and psycho somatic disorders.

"Heaven on Earth is possible only with good Health; without good health, one has to go through Hell of an Experience even in a Heavenly Atmosphere"

Prana-Vritti, is Developed after meticulous research by His Holiness Shri Aasaanji to empower the humanity with great "Health, Strength & Stamina" to achieve Success, Peace & Happiness and above all sustainable a well-being throughout the life.

NOTES FROM THE MASTER

As it is well known, every ancient Indian scripture insists on one eternal truth - Your body is the only shrine where you can experience the eternal divinity. Humans being ignorant about this gifted power spend lot of money, time and energy to create an external space for worshipping God or to experience God. The time you have spent or the space you have created is of no use unless you create the right condition for the physical body to raise your consciousness and experience oneness with the divine. Therefore, it's our primary responsibility to take good care of our body, mind & intellect which is the only source through which you can access the cosmic consciousness which will give you the power to shift every aspect of life to create a future full of peace and prosperity from now and forever.

AHAM BRAHMASMI !

www.atmayoga.in